BREAD
B·DY
SPIRIT

Finding the
Sacred in Food

Edited and with Introductions by ALICE PECK

Walking Together, Finding the Way®
SKYLIGHT PATHS®
PUBLISHING
Woodstock, Vermont

Bread, Body, Spirit:
Finding the Sacred in Food

2008 First Printing
© 2008 by Alice Peck

For information regarding permission to reprint material from this book, please mail or fax your request in writing to SkyLight Paths Publishing, Permissions Department, at the address / fax number listed below or e-mail your request to permissions@skylightpaths.com.

See pp. 187–189 for a continuation of this copyright page.

Library of Congress Cataloging-in-Publication Data
Bread, body, spirit : finding the sacred in food / edited by Alice Peck,.
   p. cm.
 ISBN-13: 978-1-59473-242-3 (quality pbk.)
 ISBN-10: 1-59473-242-6 (quality pbk.)
 1. Food—Religious aspects. I. Peck, Alice.
 BL65.F65B74 2008
 204'.46—dc22
                          2008006675

10 9 8 7 6 5 4 3 2 1
Cover design: Jenny Buono
Cover illustrations: ©iStockphoto.com/Dra Schwartz
Cover photo: ©iStockphoto.com/DNY59

Manufactured in the United States of America

SkyLight Paths Publishing is creating a place where people of different spiritual traditions come together for challenge and inspiration, a place where we can help each other understand the mystery that lies at the heart of our existence.

SkyLight Paths sees both believers and seekers as a community that increasingly transcends traditional boundaries of religion and denomination—people wanting to learn from each other, walking together, finding the way.

Published by SkyLight Paths Publishing
A Division of Longhill Partners, Inc.
Sunset Farm Offices, Route 4, P.O. Box 237
Woodstock, VT 05091
Tel: (802) 457-4000   Fax: (802) 457-4004
www.skylightpaths.com

This book is for Duane and Tyl (again).
You nourish me.

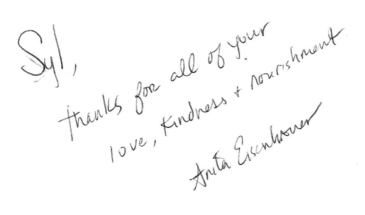

Syl,
thanks for all of your
love, kindness + nourishment.
Anita Eisenhower

CONTENTS

INTRODUCTION

People perceive food to be almost like God.

CHINESE PROVERB

Everyone needs to eat, to be nourished. It's simple. It's unending. Food presents us with a vast opportunity: through our experiences of food we can sustain a constant connection to the Sacred that pervades our lives—grace, gratitude, faith, and all the manifestations of sharing with others.

The more we consider the roles food plays in the everyday, the more remarkable it becomes, illuminating ceaseless means to examine the sublime. I think of the hugely ordinary (billions of mothers have done it) but absolutely profound and literally life-changing moment when I fed my son his first bite of rice cereal, his first solid food—his astonishment and delight at his encounter with this strange but surprisingly tasty substance. (Just imagine the privilege of getting to serve someone his or her first food ever.) I think of the grace my family recited every evening as I was growing up: *Bless this food to our use and us to Thy service.* I think about dinner parties I've given and the thrill of cooking, serving, and watching people enjoy the food I prepared.

And then I think about all the times I missed those moments by not paying attention to the poetry of the ordinary.

Looking closely at the relationship between bread, body, and spirit—the food we eat, how we eat it, and who we invite to our tables to share it—can become a framework for the study of what's sacred about a seemingly mundane part of our lives. More important, we can begin to acknowledge how food affects those around us—beginning with our immediate families, and ultimately including the entire world. I've done my best to demonstrate this universal connection to the Divine that can be fostered through food. I gathered an intentionally eclectic group of writings that explore the ways food and how we approach it—from growing it, preparing it, serving it, eating it, and sharing it—has the possibility to bring us closer to all that is holy. Writing on the subjects of, celebrating with, praying about, and ritualizing food is the stuff of every belief system. Once you begin examining the links, it's hard to look at food without seeing its spiritual significance.

As an appetizer, taste these words by cultural historian Thomas Berry:

> ... [W]e cannot be fully nourished in the depths of our being if we try to isolate ourselves individually or if we seek to deprive others of their share by increasing our own, for the food that we eat nourishes us in both our souls and our bodies. To eat alone is to be starved in some part of our being.

The "alone" Berry describes is not necessarily sitting at a table by yourself, but rather experiencing food without a sense of consideration—consideration for where the meal came from and who else is eating or not. Food has the extraordinary power to unite us with others as well as with the spiritual. It also provides a lens through which we can look inward to better understand our perceptions of the Sacred and ourselves. This is the essence of what I've tried to demonstrate in my book by juxtaposing all sorts of faith and literary perspectives.

Food ranks with love and death among the subjects most frequently written about, so if you're looking for a comprehensive volume that will tell you everything there is to know about finding the sacred in food, this is not that book. Such an enterprise would compete with the *Oxford English Dictionary* for shelf space. For that matter, I could easily compile a lengthy tome using only one ingredient as the subject, such as "finding the sacred in bread" or "finding the sacred in lemons" or "finding the sacred in chicken." Seriously.

So much has been written that I had to create limits as I looked at how writers from different spiritual backgrounds express what they find to be holy about food. I've taken engaging pieces that trace the divine elements that can be found in all aspects of food, and supplemented the selections with spiritual texts—Buddhist, Christian, Hindu, Jewish, Muslim, Native American—that address those same divine qualities. There's not a recipe in the book and I left out the almost limitless literature of cookbooks (with two exceptions: Grace Paley's introduction to the *Greenwich Village Peace Center Cookbook* and William Espe Brown's introduction to *The Tassajara Bread Book*). Likewise I steered away from (and so, barely touched on) many critical issues involving food—famines, eating disorders, labor abuses, pollution, hunger strikes—and tried to concentrate on the experience of food as a direct route to the Divine, not food as a path to another, often tremendously important, end. Nonetheless, I suspect and hope some of these larger issues will come to mind as you connect with the themes in this book.

In examining how our meals accent our faiths, often the big holiday celebrations first come to mind. Each tradition has one, from Christmas, to Passover, to Eid, to Diwali, to Vesak, to Thanksgiving—and although they all merit reflection, what really interests me is how we can find what is sublime in our everyday encounters with food. Where is God in the supermarket? Can we see the holy in a strawberry? Think about the mint we pop into our mouths without much thought as we're driving. Where did it come from? What's in it? Who made it? What about those chicken nuggets?

As I reflected on questions like those, the selections I was drawn to were remarkably diverse and ecumenical. I tried to create parallels between those pieces that will make you say, "Aha!" and those that perhaps relate to how you already perceive food—as a vehicle bringing you closer to the spiritual.

To accomplish this, my book is divided into parts. I begin with the transformation food undergoes—in the garden, at the slaughterhouse, in the preparation of food for consumption—and then move beyond to explore how food is eaten and served, and finally, partaking of and distributing the bounty. From there I shift to broader concepts—the various practices and rituals involving food, including abstaining, feasting, and sharing meals with our families, our neighbors, and our world.

Each part begins with a grace. What a fine word! Although the definition that initially comes to mind is "a short prayer at a meal asking a blessing or giving thanks," the first definition in the dictionary is really quite beautiful and integral to recognizing the Sacred in food: "unmerited divine assistance given humans for their regeneration or sanctification."

As in my previous anthology, *Next to Godliness: Finding the Sacred in Housekeeping* (SkyLight Paths), I open each part with a brief introduction—notes on the whys and hows of the pieces. I've also created titles for the passages that didn't already have them in the hopes of giving you compass points for navigating my choices. I see these titles as guideposts along this journey of contemplating and articulating the progression from bread to body to spirit—the growth from the small and tangible, its internalization, and ultimate expansion to include the sublime.

And so, like that miraculous but pure feeling of taking a first bite when you're really, really hungry, I hope this book fills you up.

Hail, hail, hail

May happiness come.

May meat come.

May corn come.

Just as farmers work

And look forward to the reaping,

So may we sit again as we are sitting now.

GHANAIAN PRAYER

Part One

THE GARDEN

ACTS OF FAITH

lanting a seed is an act of faith. It's about hope and trust. From the promise of placing a tiny kernel in black dirt, to the miraculous transformation from seedling into flower into fruit into food, to the anticipation of harvest when the miracle becomes the tangible, these same cycles of growth and change found in the garden are mirrored by many faiths.

It's wild when you think about it—a little black speck becomes a raspberry bush, a rocklike object becomes a stalk of corn. There's a logic to the botany, of course, but the poetry of the process is remarkable. Something small and mysterious evolves into something else, something beautiful that can feed people and affect its environment. From the miracle of a seed we move to the anticipation, the transformation, the fruit, and what we do with that fruit.

The simple seed embodies limitless potential, and this is a theme resonant in many spiritual traditions (think of the Garden of Eden or the Bodhi tree). This metaphor can be drawn in many directions, from self-transformation, to a small change that can influence an entire community, to ways that we can better our entire planet. Maybe it's meditation, or sitting down together for dinner as a family, or picking up litter, or fighting injustice. Each action we take begins with planting a small seed that, with tending, will bear the fruits of goodness, love, and grace.

There's a Bible verse (Mark 4:26) that sums this up nicely: "The kingdom of God is like a man who casts seed upon the soil; and he goes to bed at night and gets up by day, and the seed sprouts and grows—how, he himself does not know." This section, "The Garden: Acts of Faith," explores the essential mystery that Mark describes—the seemingly impossible transformation begun with the simple act of sowing a seed. Like the magic of a seed becoming something more, what appears to be drudgery can turn into a moment of profound connection to the Sacred. These writings speak to what we don't know as blossoms turn to fruit, and fruit becomes food. It's a tiny, accessible miracle.

Jalal ad-Din ar-Rumi, the Persian sage and poet mystic who wrote during the thirteenth century, sees sowing and consumption—the beginning and the end—as one, as a cycle: "Passing, passing / The blossom gives way to fruit." Just like the seed that develops into wine, as spiritual beings we are also always in the process of becoming: "Bread exists to be broken / To sustain its purpose." This seed could be a meditation, a prayer, a promise to do good. However it is manifested, in seed or blossom or fruit or wine, the Divine is within us.

Writing in the same century as Rumi, but from a European perspective, Meister Eckhart takes the metaphor of the seed and adds the element of responsibility to the exploration of the holy: "With a good, wise, and industrious farmer, that seed will flourish ... and the fruit would be akin to God's nature." In his simple words we can see the inconsequential as a link to the Sublime. Eckhart concludes with a message of hope, assuring us that even when the seed is obscured, the holy remains.

In Sister Miriam Therese MacGillis's article, food is more than a "metaphor for spiritual nourishment, but is itself spiritual." As she writes about her life and work as a "green nun" on Genesis Farm in northwest New Jersey, MacGillis takes Meister Eckhart's concept of "the good seed and the wicked farmer" one step further. She describes her path of "sacred agriculture" and her conviction that by tending to the earth, farmers have not only a practical, but also a spiritual role in our society. For MacGillis, cultivating the food from her farm—her garden—is "literally a manifestation of Spirit." She experiences "food as a holy mystery through which we eat ourselves into existence"— testament to the hallowed aspect of the cycle, something that conveys grace, a sacrament.

Sacrament, too, is what Episcopalian priest and sustainable food advocate Rev. Jennifer Baskerville-Burrows explores in her poetic essay about her Meyer lemon tree. As she and her husband nurture this tree and include it as part of their family, it comes to represent unity, community, and the power of love's reach—through geographic lines and despite our various backgrounds.

Writer Alison Luterman's "Every Piece of Fruit" is an epiphany that arises from considering strawberries—to reach her table, her plate, her toast, the strawberries came from somewhere and were touched by someone, perhaps someone who suffered. By considering the human condition, Luterman highlights the universal connections we share, and the influence awareness of that connection can have on our actions and choices.

Writer Kahlil Gibran's feast of faith speaks to a similar connection, even as he explores it through an apple's cycle. He writes, "And the buds of your tomorrow shall blossom in my heart...." Eating becomes an act of worship that can be sustained through the passing of the seasons both of the planet and the spirit. Gibran's words transition us from the promise of sowing seeds to the responsibility of taking and consuming life—"your blood and my blood is naught but the sap that feeds the tree of heaven."

So the beginning—the seed—is really no beginning at all. It's an endless sequence, for the end contains the beginning: the fruit bears the seed bears the fruit. The cycles of the garden, the seasons, love, and humanity, are, we come to realize, an unbroken whole.

Jalal ad-Din ar-Rumi

THE BLOSSOM GIVES WAY TO THE FRUIT

Passing, passing
The blossom gives way to the fruit,
Both are necessary.
One passes into another.
Bread exists to be broken
To sustain its purpose,
The grape on the vine
Is wine in the making,
Crush it and it comes alive.

Meister Eckhart

THE SEED OF GOD

Even pagan masters, such as Cicero and Seneca, speak of the nobility of the inner man, that is the spirit, and the worthlessness of the outer man, that is the flesh, saying that no rational soul can exist without God and that the seed of God is in us. With a good, wise, and industrious farmer, that seed would flourish all the more and would grow up towards God, whose seed it is, and the fruit would be akin to God's nature. The seed of a pear tree grows into a pear tree, that of a nut tree into a nut tree, and the seed of God grows into God. But if the good seed has a foolish and wicked farmer, then weeds will grow, smothering the good seed and pushing it out, so that it cannot reach the light or grow to its full height. But as the great master Origen says: since it is God himself who has engendered this seed, sowing and implanting it, it can never be destroyed or extinguished in itself, even if it is overgrown and hidden. It glows and gleams, shines and burns and always seeks God.

Sister Miriam Therese MacGillis

FOOD AS SACRAMENT

In 1980 I came to live and work at Genesis Farm, a 140-acre farm be-
queathed to my Dominican congregation in 1978. It was founded on a
vision of creating a space where people of good will could come to ask
the critical questions around our contemporary crises. It was to be a
reflection center where we would also grapple with the challenges of
our Western life-style, our alienation from the natural world, and the
issues of land, agriculture, and food.

Genesis Farm is a "learning center for re-inhabiting the Earth," a descriptive phrase taken from the writings of Thomas Berry. The two primary dimensions of our work are in the areas of learning and agriculture.

The learnings lead us to alter radically our perceptions of the ori-
gin and nature of the Universe as a bio-spiritual reality. We work to
heal the separation of matter and spirit, as that single human percep-
tion that has so intrinsically affected the beliefs upon which the whole
of Western culture is founded. Our programs and workshops are de-
signed to help us experience ourselves as a dimension of the Earth, and
to expand our concept of self to include our Earth self, our Universe
self, as one single reality. This is no small undertaking. Redefining
ourselves in a bioregional context has become a primary source of personal transformation. This, too, is profoundly challenging. Each of
our programs takes these learnings as its starting point.

The second major thrust of Genesis Farm is in the area of what
we now call "sacred agriculture." In the words of Vincent McNabb,
O.P.: "If there is one truth more than any other, which life and thought
have made us admit, against our prejudices, and even against our will,

it is that there is little hope of saving civilization or religion except by the return of contemplatives to the land." Laying a contemplative foundation for our work in sacred agriculture rests on two central bodies of thought that we try to integrate.

The first is the exploration of the Earth as a self-nourishing organism. This concept displaces the prevalent cultural assumption about the role of farmers as the "growers" of food. When we begin to grapple with the differences in these perceptions, it becomes obvious how enormous is the shift of consciousness demanded to transform agriculture as practiced in the industrialized world. There are scientific, educational, and economic institutions that would virtually collapse if this understanding became evident and operable in our human communities.

If we understood the Earth as a living being whose activities are to nourish, govern, learn, heal, regenerate, and transform itself, then the mystery at the heart of human existence would open up and draw us into the sacramental aspect of our lives through the most ordinary and familiar ways. The second major influence in our farming comes from the philosophy of Rudolf Steiner, a practice known as biodynamic agriculture. Steiner lived in Austria at the turn of the century. While he did not have available the insight drawn from quantum physics, or Gaia theory, or the observations of our space explorers, his knowledge of the spiritual world pervading the world of matter resulted in an approach to farming and to the nourishing function of food that is extraordinary. Since 1987 the fields and gardens of Genesis Farms have been cultivated with this biodynamic approach. The food from this garden is literally a manifestation of Spirit.

It has become clear to me that the concept of food itself is key to the transformation of our ecological crisis. Unless our human species can open itself to the contemplation of food as a holy mystery through which we eat ourselves into existence, then the meaning of existence will continue to elude us. Our present cultural experience of food has degenerated into food as fuel, for supplying the energy for our insatiable search for that which will fill the hungers of our soul. When we understand that food is not a metaphor for spiritual nourishment, but is itself spiritual, then we eat food with a spiritual attitude and taste and are nourished by the Divine directly.

From early times Western culture has carried the burden of guilt for the existence of chaos in the Universe. Only now are we realizing that the Universe was divinely organized from the beginning with chaos as an integral dimension. Our earlier perceptions have cast a shadow over the attitude with which Western peoples have "discovered" and evolved "agriculture." Feeling doomed to earn our bread by the sweat of our brow explains part of the deep, hidden rage against the natural world described by Thomas Berry. Our propensity toward favoritism has closed us off to the full diversity of nourishment offered by the Earth. It has constrained us by the narrow choices we elected in our methodology of monoculture. This clearly has shaped our present agricultural crisis.

The determination to redeem the Earth and transcend its natural limitations has played itself out in the industrialization and total mechanization of farming. The soils have been exhausted and drugged, their inner life forces depleted and poisoned, not because we are necessarily an evil species so much as that we are driven by our abstract ideas about a perfect world. We have been encultured toward an inability to experience the Universe as it actually is. We end up tearing apart the "garden planet" in our effort to redesign it. If we were to accept the Earth on the terms and under the exquisite conditions in which it continues to evolve, the role of the farmer would be raised to a most honorable and sacred human profession. Relieved of the illusions that they are manufacturing food, or that they are worthy of success to the degree that they are also economists, cosmeticists, and managers, farmers might understand themselves as acting in something akin to a prophetic and priestly role.

We need to see farmers as entering the sanctuary of the soil and engaging the mysterious forces of creation in order to bless and nourish the inner and outer life of the community they serve. Villages, towns, and cities surrounded by farms practicing sacred agriculture would begin to regain the elemental prosperity of pure air, water, and diversity, and the possibility for health and vitality. The attention farmers would pay to the rhythms of the celestial world could re-inspire the artists and poets. The music and texture of "place" would be grounded in the great seasonal cycles by which the human has been fashioned in our longing for communion with the Mystery at the heart of the world. As our culture shrinks in its inner life and rages in violence between individuals and groups, and against the whole of nature, we might do well to reflect on the meaning of food. I do not believe that we are doomed to the inevitability of "engineering" food into a state of eternal shelf life, or that we must use our most deadly nuclear inventions to irradiate our food for its immortality. These compulsive tendencies can be changed. We live in a Universe with an inner spiritual reality. There is nothing that does not participate in this deep sacramental presence. The soils, the microbes, the animals are all holy, are all revelatory. Understanding the Universe in this way has the capacity to transform our obsession with control and power.

It is my hope that the concept of sacred agriculture will find expression and authenticity on our land at Genesis Farm. By opening afresh the sacramental dimension of food, I hope to open the meaning of Eucharist and Gospel, so that we learn again to treat creation "knowingly, lovingly, skillfully, reverently" ... as a sacrament. Let contemplatives return to the land.

The Rev. Jennifer Baskerville-Burrows

LEMON LOVE

I have always believed that love will last. Love is in the realm of things sacramental and like those things that reflect the Divine life, it should hold, endure, and abide. But lemons are not like love—or so I had thought.

Some four years ago, the day after my husband and I returned from our honeymoon, we went to a garden nursery in Berkeley, California, to purchase something that I had craved almost as much as a life partner—a Meyer lemon tree. It stood all of two feet high and I had no idea whether it would bear fruit—those orangey-yellow globes of sunshine that I loved so much—but I was a newlywed and an optimist, so I brought this dwarf Meyer lemon tree into our home as a symbol of our new life together.

I knew nothing about growing lemons. My previous gardening experience amounted to a planter of spinach and pots of herbs grown on my apartment balcony. I put the little tree into a pot and rolled it out to a sunny spot in the courtyard of our apartment complex and waited. Oh, there was lots of water, worrying, and hoping too, as the summer months passed and not one bloom appeared. This was my first lesson: citrus is winter fruit. But we could be patient and wait out the cool, rainy winters of northern California.

More months passed, we moved to another apartment complex and another courtyard—one where we could look down from our balcony to see our little lemon tree. Finally, sometime in February, I heard my husband call up—"We've got lemons!" I could barely contain my excitement. I looked closely and there they were—small, green, hard—but lemons they would be. Someday.

More months passed, my husband and I began to learn the new dance of married life. We reveled in all the goodness that the Bay Area had to offer. We built great memories made of friends gathered around our table and meals lovingly prepared. Friends and family alike asked after our lemon tree as if it were a member of the family—it became that much a part of us.

More months passed, the lemons grew, and soon came an opportunity for employment back in my home state of New York. It was a great position but it pained us to think of leaving the Bay Area. Nothing worried me more than what would happen to our lemon tree. We couldn't take it with us—the harsh winters of upstate New York would do it no favors.

As one who handles sacred things for a living—freshly consecrated bread and wine, relationships tender with newness or strife—I tend to have a solid faith life. But God's presence was confirmed for me once again when our lemons became ripe enough to pick just weeks before our cross-country move. Few things taste as good as fruit lovingly tended day by day. A visit to a farm stand or a fruit orchard will confirm this. And indeed, I couldn't imagine anything more lovely than this fruit—it adorned our salads, starred in vinaigrettes, dazzled in risottos, until there were but a few left. About as many remained as our days in California.

So I did the only thing that made sense to me: I made jars of Meyer lemon curd. The day before the moving truck arrived we went to dinner with our dearest friends and I gave them each jars filled with sunshine. We also said goodbye to the tree. Its home would remain in California with someone who would love it as much as we did. We could be at peace about it.

Life in upstate New York proved to be filled with wonderful new experiences, discoveries, and friends. From time to time we would look at pictures of our Meyer lemon tree and remember. We'd think of the early days of our love (the good and the difficult). We'd think of our hopes and our longings and how much of both were lavished on our innocent lemon tree. We missed California and we missed our tree—of this there was no doubt.

Months passed. A few years passed. Nearly three years after we left California a box arrived. It was a large box and because it came while we were out of the country it wasn't opened immediately. But it was okay because as it turns out, lemons *are* like love. Our dear friend, the caretaker of our tree, had sent us fruit—beautiful, orangey-yellow orbs that brought everything back to us as if they were madeleines. So I did the only thing that made sense to me: I made jars of Meyer lemon curd in celebration of the endurance of lemons and of love.

Alison Luterman

EVERY PIECE OF FRUIT

Strawberries are too delicate to be picked by machine. The perfectly ripe ones even bruise at too heavy a human touch. It hit her then that every strawberry she had ever eaten—every piece of fruit—had been picked by calloused human hands. Every piece of toast with jelly represented someone's knees, someone's aching back and hips, someone with a bandanna on her wrist to wipe away the sweat. Why had no one told her about this before?

Kahlil Gibran

SPEAK TO US OF EATING AND DRINKING

Then an old man, a keeper of an inn, said, "Speak to us of Eating and Drinking."

And he said:

"Would that you could live on the fragrance of the earth, and like an air plant be sustained by the light.

"But since you must kill to eat, and rob the young of its mother's milk to quench your thirst, let it then be an act of worship,

"And let your board stand an altar on which the pure and the innocent of forest and plain are sacrificed for that which is purer and still more innocent in man.

"When you kill a beast say to him in your heart,

'By the same power that slays you, I too am slain; and I too shall be consumed.

'For the law that delivered you into my hand shall deliver me into a mightier hand.

'Your blood and my blood is naught but the sap that feeds the tree of heaven.'"

"And when you crush an apple with your teeth, say to it in your heart,
'Your seeds shall live in my body,
'And the buds of your tomorrow shall blossom in my heart,
'And your fragrance shall be my breath,
'And together we shall rejoice through all the seasons.'"

This plate of food,

so fragrant and appetizing,

also contains much suffering.

THICH NHAT HANH

 Part Two

FISH, FOWL, FLESH

ACKNOWLEDGING
RESPONSIBILITY

In the cosmos there are only eaters and eaten.
Ultimately, all is food.

THE UPANISHADS

Full disclosure: I've been a vegetarian for most of my life, so I came to this chapter about eating meat with limited experience, but much consideration. Being a vegetarian wasn't something I was born into, it was a conscious choice—to not take life unnecessarily—and a way my personal relationship with food connects me to the Sacred. Still, I live in a world populated primarily by carnivores and I try my best not to pass judgment. The conclusions I've reached about meat eating, and which I hope the writings that follow illustrate, are that examining our actions and taking responsibility for them is a way to discover the Sacred in everything we do (every bite, every gesture, every word, every breath, every choice), and everything we eat (every burger, every piece of sushi, every greasy pork chop). Or not.

Buddhist monk and peace advocate Thich Nhat Hanh's grace and the Native American blessing that open this section were written on different sides of the world at different times, but express the same revelation: suffering occurs so that one may eat. We as eaters should be aware of this sacrifice of life—it might be the life of a plant or an animal—but this simple awareness can expose us to concepts more far-reaching than that. Who didn't get to eat because we did? Did the piglet suffer as it was slaughtered? Did the slaughterer? Were all the parts of the lamb used? Was any wasted? How did the calf end up a steak?

Poet Nancy Willard's "A Wreath to the Fish" on her drain board takes the cosmic and makes it intimate as she considers the journey a fish has traveled before it lands in her kitchen. The fish becomes "a little martyr, a little miracle." Seeing the fish as something more than a plastic-and-Styrofoam-wrapped food product, she does as the Upanishads instruct and "worships the Divine as food."

21

In "On Murdering Eels and Laundering Swine," food writer Betty Fussell tells us, "All that lives is food for man who, dead, is food for worms. That's the deal." Drawing from biblical passages, Fussell demonstrates that killing isn't easy: eels don't go down without a fight. Laundering swine, a prettier way of saying "washing hog guts," has its own challenges. Fussell discovers that she "can turn murder into blessing by symbolic salt, but excrement into sacrament is a harder trick to turn." Ultimately, through her arm-deep understanding of the creatures she's about to eat, Fussell realizes that "no amount of murdering, no amount of laundering, will change my promised end as meat and grabby [*sic*] for rutabagas, pudding for worms."

Do we take genuine responsibility, or for that matter, any responsibility at all for where our dinner comes from? Rabbi Zalman M. Schachter-Shalomi highlights the living situations of animals before their meat reaches our cutting boards, then broadens his gaze to encompass the whole planet. In his musings on what is kosher—sanctioned by Jewish law as fit for human consumption—he asks us to examine the history of our food before it arrives at our supermarkets. Think about the cruel farming conditions, the chemicals, and the politics of countries that grow our food. In considering where the animals came from and their circumstances, Schachter-Shalomi encourages us to "reestablish our organic connection with the will of God."

Growing and raising your own food is another situation altogether, but this is just what the Kingsolver family attempted to do. In Barbara Kingsolver's essay, she writes about her family's decision to return to the land, to a life that respects the planet, and how her daughter Lily's chickens symbolize the experience. Chicken for dinner was merely chicken for dinner—until Mr. Doodle became Lily's pet. Through raising and loving chickens Kingsolver realizes that, "If we're willing to eat an animal, it's probably only responsible to accept the truth of if its living provenance rather than pretending it's a 'product' from a frozen-foods shelf." Also, it's probably best not to give the animal a first name. By participating in where their food comes from, Kingsolver and her daughter receive the bigger gift of the bounty—

knowing its origins and playing an important role in respecting the animal's life.

A remarkable insight into an animal's consciousness is demonstrated in "Tale of the Giveaway Buffalo" as conservationist and chimpanzee researcher Jane Goodall recounts a story from the Washo Indian tribe. What if an animal knows that it will be sacrificed so that people can eat? What changes if eaters understand that they will consume a sentient being? Using ritual and reverence, the Washo people elevate the meat-eating process to a whole new realm of sanctity, and the "giveaway" Goodall describes takes on an even higher level of meaning when an older buffalo actually, astonishingly, sacrifices his life for a younger animal, an action profoundly reminiscent of Jesus breaking bread with his disciples in Matthew 26:26. This experience makes Goodall "more thankful for all those that have given away to me in my lifetime and inspired to give more of myself than ever before."

Writer Michael Benedikt's prose poem "Beef Epitaph" illustrates the spiritual disconnect that happens when we separate ourselves from the sources of our food. We can lose the essences of ourselves in ignoring the relationship to the Sacred that can be found in the grocery store and at our tables. Poet Barbara Tanner Angell shifts from irony to directness in her poem "Deer Season," where the act of taking a life portrays the cycle of sacrifice and sentience. Her words awaken us to the effect understanding that cycle can have.

The pieces in this section show the sometimes bloody realities of what is on our plates, passed through the window at a drive-through, or taken out of the freezer to thaw. By unflinchingly looking at these truths we, carnivore or not, can connect to the universal, the karmic, the holy part innate to every breathing being.

A Native American Blessing

SACRIFICE

Now that I am about to eat, O Great Spirit, give my thanks to the beasts and birds whom You have provided for my hunger, and pray deliver my sorrow that living things must make a sacrifice for my comfort and well-being. Let the feather of corn spring up in its time and let it not wither but make full grains for the fires of our cooking pots, now that I am about to eat.

From the Taittiriya Upanishad

CYCLE

From food all creatures are produced
And all creatures that dwell on earth
By food they live
And into food they finally pass.
Food is the chief among beings ...
Verily he obtains all food
Who worships the Divine as food.

Nancy Willard

A WREATH TO THE FISH

Who is this fish, still wearing its wealth,
flat on my drainboard, dead asleep,
its suit of mail proof only against the stream?
What is it to live in a stream,
to dwell forever in a tunnel of cold,
never to leave your shining birthsuit,
never to spend your inheritance of thin coins?
And who is the stream, who lolls all day
in an unmade bed, living on nothing but weather,
singing, a little mad in the head,
opening her apron to shells, carcasses, crabs,
eyeglasses, the lines of fishermen begging for
news from the interior—oh, who are these lines
that link a big sky to a small stream
that go down for great things:

the cold muscle of the trout,
the shining scrawl of the eel in a difficult passage,
hooked—but who is this hook, this cunning
and faithful fanatic who will not let go
but holds the false bait and the true worm alike
and tears the fish, yet gives it up to the basket
in which it will ride to the kitchen
of someone important, perhaps the Pope
who rejoices that his cook has found such a fish
and blesses it and eats it and rises, saying,
"Children, what is it to live in the stream,
day after day, and come at last to the table,
transfigured with spices and herbs,
a little martyr, a little miracle;
children, children, who is this fish?"

Betty Fussell

ON MURDERING EELS AND LAUNDERING SWINE

Murder we must. If not cows and pigs and fish, then cabbages and rutabagas. We flay bananas, violate oysters, ravage pomegranates. Our lot is beastly and there's no help for it, for feed we must on creature kinds. Our hands are stained with carrot blood and not all the seas of Noah's Flood will wash them clean, not after God's pact with Noah: "Every moving thing that lives shall be food for you." That's a lot of territory in which to assert our puny manhood and decree that this is fit and this not, this food pure and that dirty. No, all that lives is food for man who, dead, is food for worms. That's the deal.

Some living things are harder to kill than others, even though some things beg to be killed. Snakes, for instance. Their very shape mirrors our throttled circumstances, the narrowness of our confines, the anguish of our passage. The same root, *ango*, generates *angus* (snake) and anguish (pain). The same root generates *anguilla* (eel), a fish in snake's clothing. Its snaky form makes some eaters queasy and others ravenous, but to eat an eel you must kill him first and quite deliberately, with the zeal of an ax murderer, because he is well armed against us.

I have killed many snakes in the desert when it was their life or mine, but killing an eel in cold blood, on the fourth floor, in a New York City apartment—that's different. The eel and I were already intimate, for I had carried him in my lap in a large plastic bag on the subway from Chinatown, and he had riled against my belly as if I

28

were pregnant with eels. Watching the bag slither with speed across my kitchen floor, I was afraid to deliver him. I was, in fact, deathly afraid of snakes.

My father had kept them in cages in our basement, next to the laundry tub, the newfangled washing machine, and the old-fashioned clothes wringer. Dumping laundry from tub to washer to wringer to basket for hanging on the line, I kept my eye on the snakes. Whether harmless as garters or lethal as rattlers, they were the Serpent *anguiformes*, the One cursed by God to creep without legs or wings on its belly, condemned without mercy to the darkness of a basement with a burnt-out bulb. Their skins, if you touched them, were cold as death and, though dry, wet as an oyster. Because of them I was damned, as my grandfather had read me in the Book of Genesis, "For the imagination of man's heart is evil from his youth." I was young and therefore evil. The logic was impeccable: the snake and I were kin.

Nothing in my basement past, however, had prepared me for murdering an eel. I needed time to think and threw the bag in the freezer overnight. When I opened the bag in the sink next day, he looked stone cold dead. When I turned the water on to remove the slime, he came suddenly to life. I grabbed a Chinese cleaver and tried to grab his thrusting head, but he was all muscle and I was not. With both hands I slammed the cleaver down on what might have been his neck but may have been his shoulders. A mighty whack barely nicked him. I whacked again as, tail thrashing, he tried to worm his way down the minnow-sized drain. "I'm sorry," I apologized with every whack, and I was. But I needn't have been because I had not even scotched the snake, let alone killed him.

I looked for a blunt instrument and found a wooden mallet that I used for pounding meat. I cracked the mallet on his head and the wood split, but nothing else. He was breathing heavily, gulping air that filled a pouch below his jaws. Was he strangling? I didn't want to know. Like Raskolnikov, I wanted him dead. Like Rasputin, he refused to die. I looked to the freezer for respite and held the bag open for him to slither in. He went halfway, then with a quick U-turn wrapped his tail around my arm and began to slither out. Engulfing him with a second bag, I flopped the works onto the ice trays and slammed the freezer door.

I needed time for research and reflection, my brain against his muscle. I consulted books. "To kill eels instantly, without the horrid torture of cutting and skinning them alive, pierce the spinal marrow, close to the back part of the skull, with a sharp-pointed skewer," William Kitchiner advised in the *Cook's Oracle* in 1817. "The humane executioner," he added, "does certain criminals the favour to hang them before he breaks them on the wheel." A kind thought, but what if the criminal refused to hang? Madame Saint-Ange, in *La Cuisine*, advised French housewives to grab the eel's tail in a dishtowel and bash its head violently against a stone or wall. So much for sentimental Brits.

Surely there was some practical, efficient, clean—American— way to kill. The best way to kill an eel, A. J. McClane wrote in his *Encyclopedia of Fish Cookery*, was to put him in a container of coarse salt. I poured two large boxes of coarse kosher salt into a large stockpot, pulled the eel bag from the freezer, and slid the mound of icy coils into the pot. Before they could quiver, I blanketed them with salt and waited. Nothing stirred. Salt, McClane said, also "deslimes" the eel, but my hands and clothes were already covered with an ooze that would not wash off. When I finally inspected my victim, I found the deed was done, his mouth marred by a single drop of blood.

Skinning was yet to come. McClane suggested I attach his head by a string to a nail pounded in a board. I had neither nail nor board. What I wanted was an electric 7¼-inch circular saw with a carbide-tooth blade. What I had was a pair of poultry shears. I pierced his thick hide and cut a jagged circle below his head, then scissored the length of his belly. With one hand I held his head and with the other pulled back the skin with a pair of stout pliers. It was slow work, but the leathery hide finally slipped off the tail like a nylon stocking. Naked, he was malleable as any flesh.

With one clean stroke I severed his head and hacked him into lengths. He was a three-pound meaty boy, thick and fat. He was everything one could ask for in an eel. I put him in a pot and baptized him with white wine and vinegar, vegetables and herbs, and butter whipped to a froth. He was delicious, as fat eels always are, and crowned my murderer's feast with blessing. For the order of eels are in nature born and buried in salt. Enduring a lifetime's banishment to freshwater pastures and the long journey there and back, they return to their cradle in the salt Sargasso Sea to die in a burst of sperm and roe. "It is a covenant of salt forever": God's covenant with Levi matched the one with Noah. The salt that blesses and preserves also deslimes and kills. The eel and I were bound by the same double deal. His life for mine, salt our shared salvation.

A serpent dead, however, did nothing to scotch my deeper anguish. "Shit is a more onerous theological problem than is evil," Milan Kundera wrote in *The Unbearable Lightness of Being*. "Since God gave man freedom, we can, if need be, accept the idea that He is not responsible for man's crimes. The responsibility for shit, however, rests entirely with Him, the Creator of man." If murder is man's crime, shit is not. Shit is God's joke, yet shit we must even as we feed.

What was my relation to the ten pounds of frozen hog's guts, thawing and spreading like drowned Ophelia's hair, in my apartment bathtub? The chitterlings, ten times the length of my own inner tubing, were pastel yellow, white, and pink. They spread like dubious laundry, triggering memories of washing dirty socks and underwear in the bathtubs of innumerable French and Italian hotels that invariably forbade guests to launder. With guts as with underwear, it was better to do as a French cookbook instructs, "Take the stomach and intestines to the nearest stream or river." Women once washed guts as they washed linen, rising at dawn to carry their baskets of offal to the communal gathering place, to laugh and quarrel, a medieval poet said, as they washed "inwards" at the stream.

It is laundry that connects pig's inwards to man's outwards. The ruffles on a shirtfront were once called chitterlings, "exuberant chitterlings," as Washington Irving said, "puffed out at the neck and bosom." Our foppish frills were once the ancients' omens, when offal was deemed awe-ful and the parts most worthy of the gods. A beast's inwards then put men in touch with the stars, the outermost circle of our confinement. But we who see in serpents no more than snakes, in guts no more than garbage, in destiny no more than a gambler's shake—to our narrow and straightened palates, chitterlings are the food of slaves.

I suppose it's the smell that does it, a pervasive stink that clings to hands and hair, slightly sweet, slightly sour, like dank earth turned over, like rotting bodies in a trench, like human shit. It rubs our noses in all we would deny. Washing guts, I found clusters of fat stuck to the inner lining, along with specks of what dignified recipes call "foreign matter." Some guts are thick and rubbery, others thin and limp as wet hankies. Guts are not smooth like plastic tubing, but gathered lengthwise along invisible seams to puff like parachute silk with gas. They are gathered the way a seamstress gathers cloth for ruffles. To reach the translucent membrane of the casing, I had to strip and strip again the clogging fat until, held to the light, the stretched skin showed leaf patterns, clouds, sea scum, palely mottled and beautiful. Only by laundering the guts of swine did I discover that shit comes wrapped in a layer of clouds trapped in a membrane resilient as nylon. Still, my lustrations were brief. Most of the cleansing had been done for me at the slaughterhouse, before the guts were frozen by the Gwaltney Company, a son of IT&T. The corporate master that sent me hog's guts puts satellites in space, making however inadvertently the cosmic connection of shit and stars.

From Lily of the Valley, Virginia, a slave's granddaughter told me that she cooks chitlins in their own yellow juice with onion and garlic and vinegar, until the guts are tender enough to chew. Chewy they are, rich on the tongue like all rejected vitals—heart, liver, lights, or haslet—all those messy inwards that remind us uneasily of our own. "Cut them chitlins in small lengths, or knot 'em, and cook 'em up with collards or rice in the pot of chitlin gravy, or fry 'em deep in bubblin' fat till they float up crisp and light," she said.

Even crisp and light, a little inwards go a long way. They go a long way as vitals, en route to shitty death. Bre'r hog knows better than I the rhythm that melds eating and shitting in every moving thing that lives, in the dung birth and death of cabbages and swine, men, and snakes. "We must pitch our tents in the fields of excrement," like Crazy Jane who liked the way my fingers smell, my stove, my bathtub. The smell of chitterlings clings to the air the way the taste of chitterlings sticks to the tongue. It is a lingering power that gives, my Lily of the Valley friend says, satisfaction.

But I am a child of deodorized air and Lysol drains. My pasteurized senses are not ready for the excremental smell of my bathtub. I poured "Fragrant Pine" bubble bath into the water and was ashamed to read the labeled contents: sulfates, chlorides, formaldehydes, succinates, and an ingredient called "fragrance." I am too sanitized for the fragrance of pig shit. I can turn murder into blessing by symbolic salt, but excrement into sacrament is a harder trick to turn. God owes me there. My guts are serpentine as a mess of eels, but the inward darkness of Genesis shakes out as farce. Farce is my Exodus. I know that after a lifetime's wandering through a wilderness of snakes and swine, no amount of murdering, no amount of laundering, will change my promised end as meat and grabby for rutabagas, pudding for worms.

Rabbi Zalman M. Schachter-Shalomi

ARE THEY KOSHER?

In an age of increasingly rapid technological change, the issue of what's kosher has widened its focus to an inclusive concern for the well-being of all our fellow human beings, our planet, and the entire universe. As soon as we orient ourselves to the path of planetary survival, we must ask about a whole range of things: are they kosher?

We want to know if nuclear power is kosher, and the electricity produced by it. (And what about nuclear waste, and all the other toxins with which we pollute the air, the earth, the seas, and eventually ourselves—are they clean or unclean, kosher or *treif*?)

Eggs are generally considered kosher, but what about eggs from chickens who spend their entire lives imprisoned in a cage one cubic foot in size? Food pellets are brought to them on one conveyor belt; their droppings and eggs are taken away on another. The Bible forbids us to torment animals or cause them any unnecessary grief. Raising chickens who can go out sometimes and see the sky or eat a worm or blade of grass is one thing, but manufacturing them in the concentration camp conditions of contemporary "poultry ranches" is quite another.

According to Jewish dietary laws, all fruits and vegetables are kosher. But what about green beans or tomatoes harvested by ill-treated, underpaid, and exploited migrant workers—are they kosher? What about bananas from countries ruled by despots where the workers have few rights, and the bananas are heavily sprayed with DDT, picked green, and then artificially ripened in the holds of ships by being gassed—are they kosher?

Are chemical food additives kosher? They give food a longer shelf life, but what do they do to our lives? Who really knows what all those chemicals do to our livers, kidneys, stomachs, or intestines? And artificial coloring dyes that make food look "pretty" but may cause cancer—are they kosher? And cigarettes, which we already know cause cancer, heart disease, and other health problems—are they kosher and pure?

The list of things about which we must answer the question—is it kosher?—is endless: fur from baby seals clubbed to death? Products from endangered species? The chemicals contained in many prepared foods (look at the list of ingredients on some labels)? Products or services produced at the cost of human pain and misery? Coal from strip mines that destroy the land; oil form offshore wells that pollute the seas? After a moment's thought, you can easily add to this list.

As you can see, the concept of kosher has to do with both the individual and the universe. Helping to take care of the business of the universe begins with taking care of ourselves. The Jewish tradition is very clear about this. Each of us is part of the whole, and we matter. We are therefore obliged to treat the temples of our bodies with the respect, gratitude, and even awe they deserve.

Once we have learned to care for ourselves—as individuals, as families, as groups, as an entire species of human beings—we reestablish our organic connection with the will of God. This organic connection is neither abstract nor supernatural. It is based on a functional response to the ongoing processes of the universe. To discover these processes, all we have to do is open our hearts and eyes. If there is any great heresy, it is in making ourselves opaque to the world.

Barbara Kingsolver

FREE BREAKFAST

But for some farmers on certain land, assuming that they don't have the option of turning their acreage into a national park (and that people will keep wanting to eat), the most ecologically sound use of it is to let free-range animals turn its grass and weeds into edible flesh, rather than turning it every year under the plow. We also have neighbors who raise organic beef for their family on hardly more than the byproducts of other things they grow. It's quite possible to raise animals sustainably, and we support the grass-based farmers around us by purchasing their chickens and eggs.

Or we did, that is, until [my five-year-old daughter] Lily got her chickens. The next time a roasted bird showed up on our table she grew wide-eyed, set down her fork, and asked, "Mama ... is that ... Mr. Doodle?"

I reassured her a dozen times that I would *never* cook Mr. Doodle; that was just some chicken *we didn't know.* But a lesson had come home to, well, roost. All of us sooner or later must learn to look our food in the face. If we're willing to eat an animal, it's probably only responsible to accept the truth of its living provenance rather than pretending it's a "product" from a frozen-foods shelf with its gizzard in a paper envelope. I've been straight with my kids ever since the first one leveled me with her eye and said, "Mom, no offense, but I think *you're* the Tooth Fairy." So at dinner that night we talked about the biology, ethics, and occasional heartbreaks of eating food. I told Lily that when I was a girl growing up among creatures I would someday have to eat, my mother had promised we would never butcher anything that had a first name. Thereafter I was always told from the outset which animals I could name. I offered Lily the same deal.

So she made her peace with the consumption of her beloveds' nameless relatives. We still weren't sure, though, how we'd fare when it came to eating their direct descendants. We'd allowed that next spring she might let a hen incubate and hatch out a few new chicks (Lily quickly decided on the precise number she wanted and, significantly, their names), but we stressed that we weren't in this business to raise ten thousand pets. Understood, said Lily. So we waited a week, then two, while [chickens] Jess, Bess, and company worked through their putative emotional trauma and settled in to laying. We wondered, How will it go? When our darling five-year-old pantheist, who believes that even stuffed animals have souls, goes out there with the egg basket one day and comes back with eggs, how will we explain to her that she can't name those babes, because we're going to scramble them?

Here is how it went: She returned triumphantly that morning with one unbelievably small brown egg in her basket, planted her feet on the kitchen tile, and shouted at the top of her lungs, "Attention, everybody, I have an announcement: FREE BREAKFAST."

We agreed that the first one was hers. I cooked it to her very exact specifications, and she ate it with gusto. We admired the deep red-orange color of the yolk, from the beta-carotenes in those tasty green weeds. Lily could hardly wait for the day when all of us would sit down to a free breakfast, courtesy of her friends. I wish that every child could feel so proud, and every family could share the grace of our table.

Jane Goodall

TALE OF THE GIVEAWAY BUFFALO

This story was given to me by my friend Shadowhawk, a member of the Washo Indian tribe from the Nevada River basin, and the father of a very special young man.

"A major part of a Washo's life is centered around something called 'Giveaway'—the way of all life. The two-legged, four-legged, the birds of the air, the fish of the sea, all know that to be centered they must participate in the Giveaway. Everything in our universe practices Giveaway in one way or another. Among Native Americans the spirit of giving is very important. We believe that 'without sacrifice there is no real expression of love.' We give away to friends, relatives, and even to people we may have never met before. We give away for many reasons. We give away if we feel good, or are thankful, or if someone is in need. We express thanks, or attempt to spread the good feelings we have, by giving gifts.

"This is a tale of the 'Giveaway Buffalo.' It took place three years ago on the Grand Ronde Indian reservation in northwest Oregon. It was the time of the Spring Equinox, the time of the year when the tribes gather for the most sacred ceremony of the Cheyenne, Lakota, and other plains Indians, the time of the Sundance. This is the beginning of the new year for many Native Americans.

"The Sundance is a twelve-day ceremony of sacrifice, purification, and renewal in which dancers abstain from food and water for four days, dancing from sunrise to sunset while drummers sing ancient prayers and families and friends watch (and dance) from the arbor. Before they dance the dancers and supporters go through four days of purification. The last day of the Dance is the piercing day. The Sundancers are pierced in the chest and tied by leather ropes, which are attached to the upper part of a Sacred Tree. This is done as a sacrifice to the Creator for the healing of a friend or loved one or so that next year the people will have enough to eat.

"After the Sundance is over there is a great Giveaway and a wonderful feast with all manner of good things to eat. One of the special foods at the Sundance is that of Taanka, the buffalo, the sacred one given to the people by the Creator to give life to the Nations. It was their food, their clothing, their medicine, their lodging, their tools, and more. And that brings me back to my story about the Giveaway Buffalo.

"I had been invited to attend a buffalo ceremony on the Grand Ronde. Each year a tribe or member of a tribe donates the meat and food for the Sundance, and the honor had fallen to a Lakotan friend of mine who had a herd of buffalos on the Grand Ronde reservation. A buffalo ceremony is given to ask a sacred one to Giveaway to the people, and if you've never seen one you will be hard-pressed to believe what I'm about to tell you.

"The morning of the ceremony I asked my oldest son, Washo (who was named after our tribe), if he'd like to come with me. He is a young man who loves animals more than anything else and I knew it might be hard for him to watch but I wanted him to witness what was going to happen so that he would learn what the buffalo and other animals knew, that death isn't something to be feared and that it isn't the end but rather the beginning of life.

"He was somewhat apprehensive but wanted to spend some time with me so he agreed to come along. We got to the Grand Ronde valley early in the morning just before sunrise. It was a beautiful Saturday morning with a blue sky and the sun breaking over the rim of the hills. A hawk flew overhead as we arrived at the end of the dirt road leading to a deep valley of green pasture. There was already a large gathering of men, women, and children lined up in rows of twelve across, all facing the east. They were there to sing the honoring song, the death song of thanksgiving for the one who was going to Giveaway.

"Standing in the field with a group of elders was a Lakota medicine man, his name was Sukawaka Luta (Red Horse). The sun had risen over the tops of the mountain now and the people that had gathered in the valley began to sing. The sound hung on the early morning air and echoed back from the hilltops; it was as though the whole valley was full of voices. The sound seemed to come from everywhere. They would sing for a while, then they would turn in unison, twelve across, to another of the four directions and sing again until they had sung in all four directions and they would begin again. As they sang, the buffalo herds started coming in from all areas of the pasture. As they came they formed a half-circle in front of the elders and Luta. The buffalos just stood there as the people sang.

"Washo warmed himself in the morning sun and watched and listened. He could see that Luta had a prayer stick in his right hand and in the other was a rifle. He knew it was going to be hard for him to watch an animal die, because for him all living things are family and friends, with fear and feelings. He was just eleven years old and I wasn't really sure how this was going to affect him. While I didn't want him to experience the buffalo's death I wanted him to witness the miracle of Giveaway. The people were not hunting the buffalos, they weren't going to take one, or go out and drag one in. They were waiting for one to offer himself as a gift to the people, in the same way that people may offer themselves to the Creator by giving their lives.

"All of a sudden the singing stopped, the valley fell deadly quiet, Luta raised the prayer stick and asked for the one whose turn it was to give away to come forward. A large young bull began to walk toward Luta. As he prayed, the bull walked slowly past the elders and headed straight for the medicine man. Luta handed the prayer stick to one of the elders and placed his right hand out to accept Taanka's sacrifice. When a buffalo comes to offer the Giveaway he will place his head in the hand of the medicine man and then drop his head to die. But just before the young bull reached Luta's hand an older, larger bull came from out of the middle of the herd, and running in front of the young bull he pushed him away and placed his head in Luta's hand. Some of the herd came and circled the young bull as though to hold him back.

"It was quite an amazing sight. There is no greater love than this— that a man (in this case, an animal) lay down his life for his friends. I'm not sure who learned the most that morning, Washo or myself, but I left here more thankful for all those that have given away to me in my life- time and inspired to give more of myself than ever before."

Matthew 26:26

BLESSING

While they were eating, Jesus took bread, said the blessing, broke it, and giving it to his disciples said, "Take and eat; this is my body."

Michael Benedikt

THE BEEF EPITAPH

(1) *This is what it was*: Sometime in the recent but until now un-recorded past, it was decided by certain ingenious and commercially forward-looking cattle-ranchers in a certain large, modern Western nation which prides itself on being nutritionally forward-looking, that since people are increasingly nutrition-conscious, and increasingly in-sistent that "you are what you eat," all beef cattle on the way to mar-ket were to be marked with brief descriptive tags noting the favorite food of each animal—and also stating approximately how much each ate of it. This, it was felt, would both delight the diner and comfort the nutrition-conscious consumer: people would be able to tell beforehand exactly what kind of flavor and texture of beef they were purchasing, and would always be able to secure exactly the kind of product most likely to delight their taste, since they would know a lot more than ever before about the kind of nourishment which the animal had re-ceived (it was a little like our own, well-established, present-day mod-ern American system of catering to preferences for light and dark meat in chicken by supplying each part shrink-wrapped in a separate bag in the supermarkets). The system seemed at least at first to be des-tined for success! (2) *This is how it worked*: First, on each animal's last day on the ranch, they attached the main, or so-called "parent" tag—made out according to information provided by each rancher or their hired hands or even in cases such as family farms the rancher's imme-diate family—to each head of livestock. The information contained on each tag could be counted on of course to be perfectly accurate, since it was compiled just before shipment of the animals to the slaughter-

house—during which travel time of course the animals never eat anything anyway! Just prior to slaughtering at the slaughterhouse, the "parent tags" were carefully removed; and were then mechanically duplicated, producing dozens or even several dozens of tiny labels for each animal. Immediately afterwards, at the packing plant, these miniature, or "baby" tags were re-affixed, respectively, to the appropriate bodily parts of each animal, so that virtually every section of each animal was separately and appropriately tagged—each as if with an Epitaph.

(3) But then something went wrong with this method of delighting the diner, and of comforting the nutrition-conscious consumer. At first, quite predictably, the tags came out reading things like "Much grass, a little moss, medium grain" and "Much grass, much grain, generally ate a lot." And this, as one might expect, proved (at least at first), a great pleasure to purchasers! But then tags began coming through reading things like "A little grass, a little grain, many diverse scraps from our table"; and "She was our favorite pet—gave her all we had to give"; and there was even one tag—pictured one evening around dinnertime in a close-up shot on network television news—which was tear-stained and which said, in a child's handwriting, "Good-bye, Little Blackie Lamb, sorry you had to grow up—I'll sure miss you!" And so, gradually, despite its efficiency, this system somehow ceased to delight the diner, and comfort the nutrition-conscious consumer. (4) And that's how the practice of The Beef Epitaph became a generally neglected practice over the course of time; and how the members of a large, nutrition-conscious, and otherwise generally quite sophisticated modern Western nation very much like our own, came to eat their beef—as indeed they still do today—partially or even totally blindfolded.

Barbara Tanner Angell

DEER SEASON

My sister and her friend, Johnny Morley,
used to go on Saturdays to the Bancroft Hotel
to visit his grandfather.

One autumn, the beginning of deer season,
the old man told them,

"Used to hunt when I was a boy,
woods all around here then,
but I never went again after that time ...

the men went out, took me with them,
and I shot my first buck.
It was wounded, lying in the leaves,

so they told me,
take the pistol, shoot it in the head.
I went straight up to it,
looked right into its eyes.

Just before I pulled the trigger,
it licked my hand."

This ritual is One.

The food is One.

We who offer the food are One.

The fire of hunger is also One.

All action is One.

We who understand this are One.

Hindu Blessing

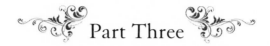

Part Three

COOKING

TAKING ACTION

You can't sort of cook. You're either cooking or not.

You have to commit to dropping the pasta into the boiling water. There comes a time to make the first cut into the melon. The chemistry begins as the yeast is stirred in. There's no turning back. Cooking is about taking action to cause a chemical or physical transformation. The pieces in this section address just that—not how to cook so much as what it means when the Sacred stops being theoretical and becomes a reality that is pertinent to our daily lives.

The process of changing comes with many labels, from "enlightenment" to "transubstantiation," but they're similar in that they each comprise the ideal of completely awakening ourselves to becoming something different—yet still the same. Just as food changes from its initial manifestation, from one substance to another—flour to cake or cabbage to slaw—we can become aware of the changes we too must undergo to discover the Divine within or for ourselves.

Zen priest and cookbook author Edward Espe Brown explains the shift from theoretical to reality in his description of how he comes alive as he cooks—just cooks. For Brown, "the Heart of Compassion enters the truth of the moment." His reflections culminate in the unambiguous question, "What's for breakfast?"

Cooking brings writer Julius Lester to the Sacred as well. He finds religion "in the knowing; it is the physicality of doing," manifested in baking *challah*. For Lester, the simplicity of preparing food reflects the miracle of everyday life.

Mary Beth Crain goes into her kitchen seeking that miracle and returns with chicken and gravy and clarity: "When food is prepared with love and joy, with the pure motive of nourishing others, it becomes a blessing for all concerned." She reaches this by putting Sri

Chinmoy's teachings of "transcendent awareness cooking" into practice and exploring how the attitudes she adopts in the kitchen have not just a spiritual but also a gustatory effect on the food she prepares.

The notion of "just cooking" can bring us to a place of enlightenment, and when that's done, what next? According to Dzogchen Buddhist teacher Lama Surya Das, in his story about Adzum Trungpa, we should just keep cooking! Once we realize our spiritual potential, what's left but to repeat the action that brought us there, so that this newfound spirituality can permeate every part of our existence?

When we satisfy one spiritual hunger, Zen Buddhists Bernard Glassman and Rick Fields write, another arises—food, power, fame, love, enlightenment. In cooking, they explain, we take responsibility for who we are feeding. The power of cooking and serving—and what they mean on a sacred level—can radiate into every aspect of our lives.

Engaging in and being present for the transformations in "just cooking" allows us to transcend experiencing the Sacred, enabling the people we feed to taste the holy as well. We can share the bounty as love, gratitude, reflection, and humility become key ingredients in any meal.

Edward Espe Brown

HOW COULD I HAVE EVER KNOWN IT WOULD BE LIKE THIS?

When we worked together in the garden, a friend told me, "Flowers are angels from distant stars come down to earth with their heavenly message. The more time you spend with them, the more you touch them, tend them, sit with them, regard them, the more you hear their message."

"And what do you listen with?" I asked.

"You listen with your eyes and nose, hands and ears."

"Yes, a whole body listening."

What to do, how to tend, how to pass on the message: star food, angel food, transfixed body, body of light, food body, cooking body. Body of bread, cake-body, body of biscuits, seed-body: the Heart of Compassion enters the truth of the moment, listening, hearing, responding.

When I cook, another body comes alive. Not the body of walking or typing, not the body of sitting or talking, but the body of cooking: a body alive to flavors and fragrance, a body ready to touch and be touched, a body which eats with eyes as well as mouth, eats and is eaten. Hands awaken, boundless with their own knowledge, picking up, handing, putting down. A whole body, nothing but food, offering.

This body cooking is also the body of my child, the body of my parents. A body holding my daughter, a body being held. Taking your tiny hand in mine, your first day of school, we walk slowly knowing life will never be the same again, and this moment is precious. My hand in yours as I breathe one last breath, nothing left to accomplish, no one left to please. I let go and relax. No one tied down, no one to be freed. No more worry about not being perfect. What's for breakfast?

Julius Lester

BRAIDING CHALLAH

I understand now.

Judaism is not in the knowing; it is in the physicality of doing.

... Friday mornings I get up early to bake two loaves of challah. I mix the flour, water, oil, salt, sugar and yeast in a bowl and then knead it for ten or fifteen minutes on one of the countertops. I am using a recipe Rabbi Lander gave me, his mother's recipe. The challah rises for an hour or so, then I knead it again, after which I brush the loaves with beaten egg yolk, sprinkle on sesame seeds to symbolize the manna God provided us in the wilderness, and bake!

When I take the loaves from the oven and stare at the mysterious beauty of their interwoven braids, they are like two songs of praise that are the color of earth, undulating like gentle hills covered with sparkling dew. I put them on bread racks to cool and then begin cooking.

Shabbat dinner is a banquet for God. If I have a hobby, it is collecting cookbooks, so I have not hesitated to buy every Jewish cookbook I can find. Cooking for Shabbat each week I am becoming a part of the Jewish people. Every dish I cook has been cooked and eaten on Shabbat for centuries. I especially like the Sephardic dishes like *fassoulia*, a simple but delicious stew of beef, green beans and pearl onions, or lamb *tagine*, a lamb stew with prunes, and almonds.

When it is time for Shabbat to begin I am tired, having been on my feet for eight hours. But I take off my apron, look at the white tablecloth, the two pewter candlesticks, tall white candles extending from each, the challah resting on a plate and covered with a white cloth, the *Kiddush* cup beside it, and the exhaustion drops from me as if it were a skin for which I have no use.

Mary Beth Crain

FOOD AND GOD: COOKING AS A SPIRITUAL CALLING

Today, cooking is the trendiest activity since the power workout. In fact, in this era of 30-minute meals, Food Challenges and mega-chefs, the kitchen seems to have supplanted the gym as the site of our primary exercise routines.

The overwhelming popularity of the Food Channel has made superstars out of plumpies like Mario Batali, Paula Deen, Ina Garten, a.k.a. The Barefoot Contessa, and those Two Fat Ladies, one of whom may she rest in peace. It has put more than a few pounds on once-diminutive Rachel Ray, and has made us wonder if skinnies like Sandra Lee and Giada di Laurentis are either bulimics or simply don't eat most of what they serve to everybody else. (Actually, I knew Sandra Lee when I lived in L.A., and I can confirm that she does eat her richest "Semi-Homemade" creations, although not in huge quantities. She also works out like a demon and has a drive and metabolism that would burn up the San Gabriel mountains if you let her loose in them.)

Yet while chefs come in all shapes and sizes, they all share one common denominator: a genuine passion for cooking and a mission to feed the world. Nothing makes a good cook happier than creating a wonderful meal and seeing the looks of joy and contentment on the faces of its recipients. When Emeril talks about how his greatest satisfaction comes from making great food for others, or Ina Garten's face lights up as she watches her guests dig in to her perfect dinners, you know it isn't just an act. In fact, there are relatively few egomaniacs on the Food Channel, in proportion to the chefs who are just having a ball doing what they truly love.

The idea of cooking as a spiritual calling has been explored in lots of movies. "Like Water for Chocolate," "Babette's Feast," "Chocolat," and "Eat, Drink, Man, Woman" are some of the film classics that explore the power of food to transmit love and transform lives. But it isn't just the food itself that does the transforming. It's the cook, whose good intentions inspire the alchemical miracle. When food is prepared with love and joy, with the pure motive of nourishing others, it becomes a blessing for all concerned.

I love to cook. I have done catering and once opened a restaurant. My greatest feat, and greatest folly, was single-handedly preparing the food for 125 people at a non-profit fund-raiser, and catering the event for free with the help of one other person. I couldn't walk for two days afterwards, but it was still a thrill, getting all those compliments from the grateful guests. I am definitely happiest when I'm bustling around my kitchen, whipping up a great meal, and having friends to dinner.

The fact that I'm diabetic is my true cross to bear. It sucks, let me tell you, but I consider myself fortunate compared to the executive chef at L.A.'s two Ritz Carltons, whom I met at a Starbucks one morning. He had just been diagnosed with insulin-dependent diabetes and was so ill that he had been hospitalized and had to take two months off work. "And when I return, what am I going to do?" he worried. "My day goes from 6 a.m. to 2 a.m. I not only create the dishes that my sous chefs prepare; I have to taste them. And the doctor says, uh uh. The most you can do is stick your little finger in it, and lick it off." Of course, this poor man also loved to eat—what chef doesn't? It was like cutting off an artist's supply to colors, or telling a pianist he had to play with his ears plugged. Talk about the ultimate curse!

Anyway, diabetes doesn't stop me from cooking and eating, but it has given me a greater appreciation for food, and for creating healthier meals that nourish the body along with the spirit. One book in particular made a huge impression on me: *The Sri Chinmoy Family Vegetarian Cookbook*. Dating from 1980, it may or may not still be in print, but if you're looking for a way to maximize both the physical and metaphysical properties of food, I'd recommend trying to hunt it down. As the preface states, "In this book, we hope to share with our readers not only our favorite foods and how to prepare them, but also our feeling for the inseparable connection between outer and inner sustenance."

Sri Chinmoy has been teaching people what I call "transcendent awareness cooking" for years. As India's Consul General in San Francisco, head of a number of spiritual/meditation centers throughout the U.S., and spiritual guide to students in some 60 countries, the 75-year-old Indian philosopher/teacher looks at food from the standpoint of higher consciousness. "The most important aspect of cooking," he maintains, "is its life-energizing reality."

Did you know that food has a consciousness? That vegetables have awareness? That you, as a cook, have the power to either positively or negatively impact others on a spiritual level through the food you prepare and serve?

"The consciousness of food depends mostly on the consciousness of the cook," says Sri Chinmoy. "It is true that food itself has its own consciousness, but since the cook is a human being, he has a more evolved consciousness than the food. So the cook can transform the consciousness of the food if he/she wants to do so. He can add to the consciousness of the food, or he can even bring the consciousness of the food into his own consciousness for enlightenment."

What attitudes should we adopt while cooking? Sri Chinmoy advocates cultivating "an innocent feeling, along with purity" when cooking for children, a "very dynamic quality" when cooking for adults, and a "soft and tender feeling" when cooking for the aged. Regarding the latter, he adds, "You can try also to have the feeling that you are helping the old people to gain new life."

And in Sri Chinmoy's kitchen, cleanliness is definitely next to godliness. "Cleanliness is of paramount importance, purity is of paramount importance, and good feelings toward the pots and pans are of paramount importance," he instructs. "Everything is of paramount importance from the beginning to the end when you cook." Talk as little as possible while cooking; should you happen to interact with anyone who may not be so highly evolved, you run the risk of transmitting "lower consciousness" to the food. Sri Chinmoy also suggests that we adopt a "meditative consciousness" while preparing a meal, and that we meditate on our food before eating it. "If we meditate before we eat, then God's compassion descends on us, and His compassion is nothing short of energizing power. So, along with the material food, if we can receive energizing power, then naturally we will get double benefit from the food."

I gave Sri Chinmoy's advice a try some years back, when I decided to cook a "higher consciousness" Indian meal. Now, I am, if I say so myself, fairly accomplished in the art of Indian cookery. Once, during a period of culinary fanaticism, I even made my own *garam masala* (curry powder), grinding up about 20 different spices by hand with a mortar and pestle. For this particular meal, I used a few tasty recipes from the *Family Vegetarian Cookbook*, along with some of my own. And for the first time in my life, I cooked with not only love, but with gratitude and humility as well.

Whereas before, cooking had been both a pleasure and an ego trip, for this meal I left my ego behind. I concentrated on my breath until I achieved a peaceful rhythm in the chopping of the vegetables. I thanked God for the food, and the food for giving us nourishment and new life. I worked not at my usual bustling pace, but with a happy serenity. And something like a miracle began to take place.

The kitchen seemed to be glowing, along with me. I had never had so much fun preparing a meal. Energy filled the room along with scents exotic and intoxicating. Everything went so smoothly that the dishes seemed to prepare themselves.

And the proof was in the rice pudding. My guests beamed as they wolfed down the potato and pea *samosas*, the cauliflower curry, the homemade apricot chutney, the chicken *makhani*, the yogurt *raita* and the *dal pakora*. The table seemed to pulsate with something more than simple gustatory satisfaction—something like unconditional love. Even though several people had brought friends whom I'd never met, a peculiar warmth overtook us, the feeling that we were all one.

"This is the best Indian food I have ever had!" exclaimed Daniel, an authority on ethnic cuisine.

"This is the best meal I have ever had!" said his wife.

And I think it was the best dinner I ever made. Even though it took place 19 years ago, I have never forgotten it. The memory still pushes my bliss button.

I feel, however, that I must issue a warning: cooking with love doesn't always bring great results. Over the holidays I got an old *American Home Magazine* from 1937, in which I found, of all things, an ad for Royal Baking Powder featuring a recipe from none other than the mother of famed aviatrix Amelia Earhart. For some odd reason I was entranced by the tinted color photo of white-haired old Mother Earhart, looking maternal and saintly, presenting her beautiful platter of fried chicken, gravy, and biscuits made with foolproof Royal Baking Powder. The promo read, "'Amelia's Favorite Dish is My Fried Chicken and Biscuits!' Says the Mother of the World's Most Famous Woman Flyer."

I think I was intrigued for three reasons. The first was that the issue was dated March, 1937, two months before Amelia Earhart's fateful final flight. What a collector's item!

The second was that the food looked scrumptious. And the third was that Mother Earhart looked like the embodiment of the loving cook. Damn, that ad worked! Suddenly, although I'd never made either fried chicken or biscuits in my life, I had to make Mrs. Earhart's.

I invited my own mother over for the grand occasion. I was so excited! That afternoon I cooked with love, joy, and anticipation. I coated the chicken with flour and egg and prepared it just the way Mother Earhart said to—frying it in oil first, and then cooking it over a low flame for 45 minutes to an hour. I made the biscuits, and then it was time for the gravy, which was to be made from the chicken drippings.

Well. The drippings were black and burned, the gravy turned out gray and revolting, and some of the chicken was still slightly red inside, even after an hour's cooking. The biscuits were OK, but nothing to write home about. The only thing that was edible was the frozen corn that I'd nuked.

I had never before in my life made such a total, unmitigated disaster of a meal. Even my Chihuahua, Truman, turned up his nose at the chicken and stared at me as if to say, "And WHAT the HELL is THIS?"

"This corn is delicious!" my mother kept saying, as she pushed the rest of the meal to the far end of the plate. "And the chicken is very good too."

"No it isn't!" I snapped. "It's disgusting!"

"Well, it isn't your best," she agreed.

At least there was dessert to look forward to—my famous pumpkin cognac pie. This is a pumpkin pie made with four eggs, heavy whipping cream, condensed milk, pecans, spices, candied ginger, and cognac. To die for. I'd been making it for, like, 20 years. Only this time it turned out too heavy on the cognac.

"This pie is sort of bitter," my mother announced tactfully.

I couldn't figure out how the whole thing happened. Me, the great cook, creating such a fiasco. I finally decided that maybe God had decided to spare us. High food consciousness or not, that meal would have put our cholesterol on Mars.

There is a happy ending to my night of humiliation, though. I decided to bake the chicken for another hour, and it turned out great. Then I threw out the gravy and made one of my own, using a white sauce, paprika, salt, pepper and country sausage. It was a definite improvement and I re-served the meal to friends with happy results.

Anyway, the next time you're making dinner, try adding the extra ingredients of love, joy, and gratitude, with a dash of humility thrown in. Treat the food and all your utensils with love and respect. Work slowly and serenely, and meditate on all you have, and all you are about to give. Involve your kids in the process, too. Serve the meal with a big smile, say grace or have a moment or two of silence before you eat, and remember Sri Chinmoy's words:

"Because food is life and life is God, both food and God are one."

Lama Surya Das

KEEP COOKING

There is a great story about a cook in Adzum Trungpa's tent camp. Adzum Trungpa was a great Master, and one day his cook, who was unlettered and untrained, burned his hand in the fire and "woke up." He came running to the master and told him what he had realized.

Everything fell apart in that moment of burning his hand; he had a total *satori* [enlightenment] breakthrough and non-dual experience. He realized who he was and the nature of all things. The master said, "That's it!" And the cook said, "Now what?" And the master said, "Keep cooking."

That cook became a great yogi, and he just kept cooking. But he had that big view, which is not intellectual. It's not a philosophical view. It's your intuitive highest wisdom. It's your gestalt, your overview, which is pre-thought, really. It's how you see the world.

Bernard Glassman and Rick Fields

FLOUR, WATER, AND DETERMINATION

... During meditation retreats, we ate our meals in the *zendo*—the meditation hall—so that even eating became part of our meditation. Before eating, we offered some food to the Buddha, the teaching, and the community. And after each meal, we offered leftovers to the hungry ghosts.

In Buddhism, the hungry ghosts are pictured as miserable creatures that have huge, swollen bellies and needle-thin necks. Even though they are surrounded by food, they can never satisfy their hunger or thirst because they can eat or drink only one drop of food at a time. Their necks are thin as needles because they are so caught up in their conditioning that they can't accept or appreciate the food that is actually in front of them.

Actually, we are all hungry ghosts. It's a metaphor for the part of us that's unsatisfied. Because of attachments and our conditioning, we miss the food and drink that's right in front of us. In fact, the ingredients we need to make a meal that will satisfy us are all right here. But we refuse to accept the food that's offered. We get taken over by the feeling that we can't do what needs to be done. So we're always looking for something we don't have. Somehow we can't just say, "Let's take all this and make a wonderful feast." It all comes down to a very human habit: we're always looking for something beyond what is right in front of us.

Hungry ghosts manifest themselves in all sorts of ways. I myself experienced the immense hunger that we all have one morning while I was riding in my car pool to work. I had been practicing meditation intensively during the early mornings when I suddenly realized the universality of hunger. I felt this great hunger all around me. I saw that even though there is enough food in our society to feed everyone, many, many people hunger for food. I saw that even though some people have more than enough food, they hunger for power. I saw that some of us thirst for appreciation or fame. Others are starved for love. And spiritual seekers, including Zen students, crave enlightenment.

As soon as I felt this great thirsting, I made a vow. I vowed to dedicate my life to offering the supreme meal to all of us hungry ghosts in the ten directions.

This is the vow of the Zen cook. In Zen, a vow is not something we promise to do and then feel bad or guilty about if we don't accomplish it. Rather, a vow is an *intention* to do something.

Many of us think we have to limit our meal because the ingredients we have on hand—whether food, money, time, talent, intelligence, or energy—are limited.

But a vow is not limited, either by space or time. We can make our vows as small or as large as we want. We can make a vow to feed one person, for instance, or we can make a vow to feed hundreds or thousands of people. We can vow to build housing for one homeless person or for hundreds or thousands of families. We can even vow to end hunger or homelessness. The only thing that limits our vow is our imagination.

But even though a vow has no limits, a vow has a very practical function: it's like a compass that shows us the direction to go in and that keeps us on course. But a vow by itself is never enough. By itself, a vow is all potential. It's like yeast or a starter. But if we want to see our vow manifest in the world, if we want to bake a real loaf of bread, one that we can eat ourselves and serve to others, we have to add flour and water and knead them all together. We have to add determination.

When we add determination, vision takes on a life and force of its own. The loaf of bread we imagined comes out of the oven, ready to eat.

Salutations!

O Merciful God who provides food

for the body and soul,

you have kindly granted what is spread

before us. We thank you.

Bless the loving hands that prepared this meal and

us who are to enjoy it, please.

Homage, homage,

homage to thee!

TAMIL GRACE

Part Four

SERVING

NURTURING

When I've attended retreats at a Buddhist monastery, the element of work practice I've loved the most and found hugely challenging has been serving food. At first it was scary and a bit tricky, bowing low with a heavy steaming bowl of porridge or vegetables held high over my head, making it back up, navigating my way down the narrow aisles of cushions, bowing to each person, then, finally, balancing on my knees to serve them. A teacher told me that as I served I should clear my mind and connect with each individual I was presenting the food to *as if I was giving them the very last meal he or she would ever eat*. So powerful ... Think about it as you pour a bowl of cereal for your child, parcel out some mashed potatoes in a soup kitchen, or a waiter refills your water glass.

The very simple act of serving—bowing to the person who is directly in front of us, just there—becomes a profound and intimate act of nurturing that unites us first with the person we offer sustenance to, but ultimately to everyone, everywhere, as highlighted by the Buddhist meal gatha. It's all about taking care of each other as if this were our very last opportunity.

Martin Buber, the Viennese religious philosopher, initiates the conversation of the experience of serving food as a path to realizing the Sacred in his story of the Zaddik of Berditchev, who was able to establish "sublime unions" and make "His meal ... a sacrifice, his table an altar." Likewise, Brother Lawrence, in his seventeenth-century reflections, encourages us to "Turn the cake that is frying on the pan for the love of Him...." For these authors, it's not just about using food to nurture peoples' physical bodies, but also discovering, as Guru Gobind Singh suggests, the holiness within it—and themselves.

Author Diane Ackerman takes a simultaneously poetic and anthropological approach to serving as she addresses the symbolic act of offering food to others—a gesture as old as humankind and as pertinent today as in the ancient times, when our rituals of food and the serving of food took root. She writes that, "In hard times, or in the wild, [the action of serving] says: *I will endanger my own life by parting with some of what I must consume to survive*. Those desperate times may be ancient history, but the part of us forged on such trials accepts the token drink and piece of cheese and is grateful." Taken in spiritual terms, we can see the sacrifices that come from love and from letting go of the importance of the self as a way to exalt those we care for.

Feeding others is an integral part of all religions and all cultures, and it even becomes a sacramental action. Considerations of the Sikh community kitchens—*langars*—as well as Zen Master Dogen's advice on how to share all offerings are two such means to recognizing the interconnectedness of all beings and nourishing (and thus nurturing) the "sacred body." Both perspectives embrace writer Jacqueline Kramer's quite literal nourishing of the sacred body as she reflects on breast-feeding her daughter and the "warm sweet milk" that provides her child with—beyond antibodies and physical sustenance—"love and reliability" as well as "warmth and connectedness."

Modern life presents plenty of opportunities to practice the power of tending to others at our tables, and writer Amanda Cook accepts this "vital responsibility" of feeding those we love, especially when it is done with clarity and intention. Food and the spirituality of food aren't just about the farmer, religious authorities who determine it *halal* or kosher, the greengrocer, or the chef; they are about the waitress in a diner who brings you an egg salad sandwich, about UNESCO workers doling out rice, about a mother serving the first lucky piece of birthday cake.

By serving food to others, we nurture them, to be sure. In so doing, we are simultaneously tending to the Sacred within ourselves and our world. What an honor!

BUDDHIST MEAL GATHA

First, seventy-two labors brought us this food.
We should know how it comes to us.
Second, as we receive this offering, we should consider
whether our virtue and practice deserve it.
Third, as we desire the natural order of mind, to be free
from clinging, we must be free from greed.
Fourth, to support our life we take this food.
Fifth, to attain our Way we take this food.

First, this food is for the three treasures.
Second, it is for our teachers, parents, nation, and all
sentient beings.
Third, it is for all beings in the six worlds.
Thus we eat this food with everyone.
We eat to stop all suffering, to practice good, to save all
sentient beings, and to accomplish our Buddha Way.

Martin Buber

HIS TABLE AN ALTAR

It is told of the Zaddik [righteous one] of Berditchev that while he was still young he was once staying with his friend, the Rabbi of Nikolsburg, and that while he was staying with him, he caused general offence [*sic*], because he went into the kitchen dressed in his prayer shawl and with the double phylacteries on his forehead, and asked after the preparation of the food; and also because he would enter into talk with the most worldly man about all kinds of apparently idle things, even in the house of prayer; that was profanation of the sacred garments, profanation of the sacred place, profanation of the sacred hour, and it was as such thrown up against him. But the Master said, "What it is only in my power to do for three hours during the day, this man is able to do all day long, he can keep his mind collected, so that he establishes sublime unions also by the talk that is counted for idle." The central desire of the *zaddik* is to hallow that which is worldly. His meal is a sacrifice, his table an altar.

Brother Lawrence

LOVE IS EVERYTHING

In the way of God *thoughts* count for little, *love* is everything.

Nor is it needful ... that we should have great things to do.... We can do *little* things for God; I turn the cake that is frying on the pan for the love of Him....

Guru Gobind Singh

TO FEED A HUNGRY MOUTH
IS TO FEED THE GURU

A Sikh visiting another Sikh's door must be served food, without hesitation or delay.

To feed a hungry mouth is to feed the Guru.

Diane Ackerman

ACCEPTING

If an event is meant to matter emotionally, symbolically, or mystically, food will be close at hand to sanctify and bind it. Every culture uses food as a sign of approval or commemoration.... Jews attending a Seder eat a horseradish dish to symbolize the tears shed by their ancestors when they were slaves in Egypt. Malays celebrate important events with rice, the inspirational center of their lives. Catholics and Anglicans take a communion of wine and wafer. The ancient Egyptians thought onions symbolized the many-layered universe, and swore oaths on an onion as we might on a Bible. Most cultures embellish eating with fancy plates and glasses, accompany it with parties, music, dinner theater, open-air barbecues, or other forms of revelry. Taste is an intimate sense. We can't taste things at a distance....

... Speaking into the perforations of a telephone receiver as if through the screen of a confessional, we do sometimes share our emotions with a friend, but usually this is too disembodied, too much like yelling into the wind. We prefer to talk in person, as if we could temporarily slide into their feelings. Our friend first offers us food, drink. It is a symbolic act, a gesture that says: This food will nourish your body as I will nourish your soul. In hard times, or in the wild, it also says: I will endanger my own life by parting with some of what I must consume to survive. Those desperate times may be ancient history, but the part of us forged on such trials accepts the token drink and piece of cheese and is grateful.

HOW TO SHARE ALL OFFERINGS

When the food has been cooked, examine it, then carefully study the place where it should go and set it there. You should not miss even one activity from morning to evening. Each time the drum is hit or the bell struck, follow the assembly in the monastic schedule of morning zazen and evening practice instruction.

When you return to the kitchen, you should shut your eyes and count the number of monks who are present in the monk's hall. Also count the number of monks who are in their own quarters, in the infirmary, in the aged monk's quarters, in the entry hall, or out for the day, and then everyone else in the monastery. You must count them carefully. If you have the slightest question, ask the officers, the heads of the various halls or their assistants, or the head monk.

When this is settled, calculate the quantities of food you will need: for those who need one full serving of rice, plan for that much; for those who need half, plan for that much. In the same manner you can also plan for a serving of one-third, one-fourth, one-half, or two halves. In this way, serving a half portion to each of two people is the same as serving one average person. Or if you plan to serve nine-tenths of one portion, you should notice how much is not prepared; or if you keep nine-tenths, how much is prepared.

When the assembly eats even one grain of rice from Luling, they will feel the monk Guishan in the tenzo, and when the tenzo serves a grain of this delicious rice, he will see Guishan's water buffalo in the heart of the assembly. The water buffalo swallows Guishan, and Guishan herds the water buffalo.

Have you measured the rice correctly or not? Have the others you consulted counted correctly or not? You should review this closely and clarify it, directing the kitchen according to the situation. This kind of practice—effort after effort, day after day—should never be neglected.

When a donor visits the monastery and makes a contribution for the noon meal, discuss this donation with the other officers. This is the traditional way of Zen monasteries. In the same manner, you should discuss how to share all offerings. Do not assume another person's functions or neglect your own duties.

When you have cooked the noon meal or morning meal according to the regulations, put the food on trays, put on your *kashaya*, spread your bowing cloth, face the direction of the monks' hall, offer incense, and do nine full bows. When the bows are completed, begin sending out the food.

Prepare the meals day and night in this way without wasting time. If there is sincerity in your cooking and associated activities, whatever you do will be an act of nourishing the sacred body. This is also the way of ease and joy for the great assembly.

Jacqueline Kramer

WARM SWEET MILK

M. F. K. Fisher, in *The Art of Eating,* says, "There is a basic thought-fulness, a searching for the kernel in the nut, the bite in honest bread, the slow savor in a baked wished-for apple. It is this thoughtfulness that we must hold to, in peace or war, if we may continue to eat to live." When I am oversaturated with anything in my life I find it difficult to share this lesson with [my daughter] Nicole. Simplicity always makes me appreciate the small things in life. [My first formal spiritual teacher] Ina taught me that not taking things for granted creates reverence. These are the lessons I wish to share with Nicole.

My first meal was warm sweet milk from my mother's breast. As I drank my mother's milk I felt her soft skin and smelled her familiar comforting fragrance. Her milk had the perfect composition of fat, sugar, and other nutrients for my growing body as well as antibodies to protect me from infection when I was so vulnerable. I learned to trust as I nursed at my mother's breast. My mother taught me love and reliability as she generously created my meal within her body.

I nursed Nicole for over a year. Nursing was painful at first. My baby sucked so hard that she tore my nipples open. I was committed to giving Nicole the best start I possibly could, and that meant nursing her. After much pain and frustration I admitted that I needed help and called the La Leche League. They showed me how to heal my nipples and the best way to hold my baby to avoid the problem I was having while nursing her. After a couple of months of pain at each nursing, my nipples healed, and the nursing experience became one of the most intimate, sweetest exchanges I've ever known. It was a rocky start, but I'm so grateful I hung in there and got to enjoy the warmth and connectedness of nursing my baby.

Milk was the last nourishment taken by the Buddha before sitting under the bodhi tree prior to his full enlightenment. The story goes that in his search for enlightenment the Buddha experimented with a number of austere forms of practice prescribed by the gurus of his time. He practiced self-mortification, denying the body food and sensual pleasure in an attempt to let go of his attachment to the physical body. In this dualistic frame of mind he considered the body a distraction, at cross purposes with the mind, a hindrance to enlightenment. He punished his body by holding his breath till near death, by staying out in the burning sun, and by eating once every other day. His once robust body became emaciated. One day he collapsed and was found by a shepherd who nursed him back to health. The Buddha, realizing the wisdom of the middle path, discontinued the practice of self-mortification and regained his vitality.

Anyone who has followed a spiritual path knows how easy it is to get so involved in the mental aspect of the spiritual practice that we neglect the physical. We forget that there is only one spiritual force, which takes an infinite number of forms, and that any appearance of duality is illusion. Our bodies are also expressions of that one spiritual force. Since Nicole's birth I have come to realize that my body is Spirit in form, the Word made flesh. The miracle of birth enlightened me to the miracle of the human body, and I experienced a deep heartfelt desire to mindfully care for my own and Nicole's body with awe and awareness. We don't need to create duality or conflict in relation to our physical and spiritual needs, for they are nothing more nor less than different forms of the same energy.

In the neighborhood where the Buddha was building up his strength there lived a woman called Sujata. Sujata vowed that if she bore a son she would make a special food offering to the deity of the nearby banyan tree, a tree that was regarded with reverence in India at that time. She milked one hundred cows and fed fifty cows on this milk. Then she milked these fifty cows and fed twenty-five on this milk, and on and on until she was left with the milk of eight cows. She used this milk to make a rice dish and brought it to the banyan tree. There, under the tree, she found the beautiful golden-hued Buddha. Upon seeing him Sujata knew that this golden figure was divine, and she offered him the milk-rice, saying, "Venerable Sire, whoever you may be, god or human, please accept this milk-rice, and may you achieve the goal to which you aspire." The Buddha ate the milk-rice, washed the bowl, and placed it in the water of the nearby river to float away, saying, "If today I am to attain full enlightenment, may this golden bowl swim upstream." It did, he did, and the rest is history.

Amanda Cook

SUGAR-FROSTED MEMORIES

Serving is a complicated business, because in the modern world it oc-
cupies the broad spectrum of tight orange shorts accompanied by a
tray of beer, a man dressed in a full vested suit presenting warmed
rolls off polished silver, and a pearl-adorned Grandmother dishing out
trifle. For most families sitting down to a meal, the server is often the
preparer or at least the purchaser, the glue of the household, the person whose unnoticed efforts bring the family together on a regular
basis. They gather and finesse all the bits and pieces that make a meal
an event and then present them as if they always co-existed. They are
not well rewarded for these tasks, but without them the system of easy
togetherness would fall apart; bellies would ache, and plates would be
empty. The efforts of the server are the unseen steel girders that support the light, airy architecture of a Sunday evening dinner.

Many people don't like to serve; they find it demeaning or beneath them. Food service is worth less than minimum wage in the
marketplace, and food servers sometimes subsist on tips. The only job
that pays less is motherhood. People do not get far without the atten-
tive care of mothers or without the energy-giving sustenance of food.

Serving deserves recognition; I see a vital responsibility, an opportunity to send someone out into the day knowing that they are loved
and cared for. With the right type of food being served, lives can literally be saved and good life habits formed. Serving is not a task to take
lightly even though it's often forgotten.

I serve my family on a regular basis, and I find a soon-empty plate
or a smile of delight reward enough on most nights, or mornings. A

peeled and sliced plate of apple with a teaspoon of brown sugar makes my six-year-old smile as if it was an Easter Bunny morning. Serving is an art, but like all things now silently mis-classified as "woman's work" its value is being forgotten. All things are not created equal, and how boring would it be if they were: Dads are great but they're not Mothers, just as bottles can be substituted for breasts but they really aren't the same. In our speedy world of fast food and prepared foods we have forgotten the love that can be delivered on a plate of china by a kind hand. There are always substitutions available, but like fake sugar there may be harmful side effects down the road.

I first observed the flair of good serving from my late Grandmother, a woman who understood that gently placing a warm plate of food in front of a guest or family member had value.

She was the kind of Grandmother you read about in storybooks; she made me fancy pleated dresses in my favorite colors and smothered me with love and let me eat sugarcoated corn flakes when my mother wasn't around. She seemed to survive on black coffee, generous amounts of cigarettes, and her daily fix of *The Young and the Restless*. She always had at least one package of butterscotch Lifesavers in her large leather purse, but I rarely saw her eat them. I always felt like she had grown up with very little and so she was stringent with herself. I did see her eat plain toast several times in the very early morning. She never laid a plate down sharply or rushed off in a huff. She enjoyed the process, understood its importance and felt comfortable in her servitude.

Grandmother never ate a meal, though food preparation occupied a good portion of her day. Occasionally I would see her sip the borscht or nibble the beet salad with the dressing that would quickly turn pink, but that was it. You could tell the tip of the spoon filled with broth was not about filling herself up, she was making sure she didn't need to add more salt or a dash of paprika. It amazes me still that she would spend almost an entire day in the kitchen for a meal that would last just slightly over an hour. I don't remember her ever sitting at the dining room table, although she'd always set a neat and tidy place for herself; it always remained unused. Instead she was in motion, bringing the next course, tending to the bread bowl or preparing someone a new drink. She enjoyed being in her kitchen, the stove was her control panel and the cutting board her easel. The dining room belonged to Grandpa, she was there to make things run smoothly for him and whomever they were entertaining. Don't let his act fool you though, she was the one holding the ladle of power. Grandpa would hold court while she tended to people's needs with an understated perfection.

But then she grew up in an era of serving. Thinking back now, if [*sic*] may have been simply circumstances that created this mastery of serving; the combination of her heritage, and the role of wife, first instilled in the forties, to a successful and demanding man. I was only ten when she died of cancer so I was never old enough to ask her why she did all that she did, in such a calm and caring way—or really to even think of the question—but I could tell she loved me by how she buttered my toast and laid the sauce on my noodles. Every single action was coated with intentional care.

Her talent for serving did not only extend to Sunday dinners; my peanut butter sandwiches with grape jelly were always made with creamy peanut butter. She knew the crunchy kind made me think I was eating bugs. She would spread it on just thick enough that I wouldn't need a sip of milk after each bite. She always cut my crusts off, my mother would shake her head and tell her not to spoil us, but she'd just say, "Grandmothers are supposed to spoil," and cut off the darker crusts, and save them for Clancy the dog. I always hoped my mom was jealous; I imagined her eating sandwiches with big thick crusts, and nutty butter—I felt lucky.

When we stayed over at Grandma's the best moment of the day was our late afternoon snack. Grandma would turn on the television, which we didn't have at home, and put the channel to her favorite soap. My older sister and I were each given a gigantic bowl of Fruit Loops, Sugar Crisps, or some other equally unhealthy but tasty cereal, from the too-high-to-reach cupboard. Then two little girls were allowed to lay [*sic*] on their bellies, jam big spoons into their mouths and watch the shenanigans of Genoa city. It was her only time "off" every day, but she'd always get up to refill our bowls without hesitation.

Her entire existence revolved around the importance of serving. Quite simply Grandpa brought home the bacon and she made sure it was cooked right and served on a pretty plate. She had a dark-colored dressing gown that she lived in for a good part of the day, then sometime after lunch she and it would disappear, and she would come out of her room dressed, combed, and ready to shop. She drove a burgundy Cadillac convertible and zoomed to the local market with a silk scarf tied around her head to protect her tidy hair. First stop was the butcher: tact and compliments meant she always got the best cuts for the best price. It was important that Grandpa arrive home to a meat-and-potato dinner. He was Irish and he expected food that could fill his belly. A few minutes before he would arrive home, she would smoke a cigarette, chew a piece of mint gum, then apply a very red lipstick, tidy her hair and take her apron off her conservative dress. She was beautiful with her almost black hair, olive skin and red lips.

She could hear his car coming down the long driveway and would open the door for him, take his hat, make him comfortable and get him a drink. Then she would disappear into the smells in the kitchen. She never asked us to help her, though we liked to. She considered the kitchen her room and didn't really like other people to interfere or disturb her cupboards. She was a quiet woman and this role allowed her to be involved in dinner parties without really having to participate in sometimes-lively conversations. Grandpa was the talker and she would listen with head tilted, lips slightly apart. She could always "escape" to the kitchen.

I, too, enjoy having people to my table and sharing my food, I don't mind spending a good portion of my evening warming sauces and getting a new fork or a dollop of this and that. In truth, for people I like or love I really enjoy it; when something is so good a guest will try to sneak a spoonful from a neighbor or off my plate and conversation is fun. There is a simple joy in knowing you can make someone else have a moment off, a time of pure joy, as tastes dance on their tongue and they have to do nothing but receive it. It also allows me to escape the table if I ever feel the need. "Oh I just need to check on the dessert" can really mean, I need some quiet time. A sip of wine alone in an otherwise muddled day.

Service can be seen as a lowly place, but in my eyes it is not. Serving is a place of control, which is probably why both my Grandmother and I enjoyed it. You set the tone, the timing, and the dance of the meal. If you're lucky enough to have someone in your family who serves your food with warmth and love and no expectations, the next time you have the plate rested in front of you—smile. We don't always need to hear it; a verbal thanks can seem forced or make the giving awkward, but seeing the thanks is always nice.

For me, the ultimate privilege is to serve someone birthday cake. I will only serve cakes that I have made myself from scratch. No store-bought cake, fancy or not will ever be the same as a cake iced by a person who cares enough to mix it all together—real vanilla, fresh eggs, in a flavor that is personal to them. In the end, serving is important because it is so personal. You are giving someone their sustenance, their energy, and, when done with intention, a little slice of joy.

Bless our hearts to hear

in the breaking of bread

the song of the universe.

FATHER JOHN GIULIANI

Part Five

EATING

BEING PRESENT

All the religion of sowing seeds, acknowledging life, preparing, and serving, reduces to this: food is for eating.

After the planting and the cooking and the careful placement of plates on the placemats, comes time for the meal. We show up for dinner—not just for ourselves, or the people at our table, but for the whole universe. It's simple and yet vast. No matter what happens, we have to eat, and different writers find different avenues to discover and share the Sacred in what's for supper. The pieces in this section aren't as much about savoring fabulous flavors as about tasting every bite of the meal that is our lives.

First, grace, in whatever form that may take. Just as we sit down to eat, it's critical to recognize those who won't get to eat and appreciate the gift of food on our tables. Hunger is a pure and brutal reality for millions of people. As we see how our meals sustain us spiritually and our spirituality sustains our meals, it's essential that we explore how we can nourish others physically so that they too, as Rabbi Karyn D. Kedar writes, can "know the feeling of a second helping." After recognizing the hunger, we need to take action. Ensuring that others can eat may be one of the most effective means of feeding our own souls—it's certainly a practice encouraged by every belief system, an important touchstone on every spiritual route.

As she examines consciously eating, poet Julia S. Kasdorf charts the path of our meal from the garden to the cutting board. She says that the onion is "not about religion," but as it becomes a metaphor for salvation, we recognize that it *is* religion—there's no separation. Through the onion, through "tasting grace, layer by layer," Kasdorf demonstrates that it's not all about the stuff, but about being right where you are.

Writer and farmer Wendell Berry should be called the master chef of finding the Sacred in food—so many of the authors and teachers I encountered were inspired or informed by his writings on what's holy about agriculture, cooking, eating, and serving. Berry's "The Pleasures of Eating" gives practical ways we can elevate the act of eating to the sublime, ways of "restoring one's consciousness of what is involved in eating" and "reclaiming responsibility for one's own part in the food economy." His essay ends with the reminder that this simple action of consciously and intentionally eating the food on our plates is not only a responsibility but a pleasure as well: "perhaps the profoundest enactment of our connection with the world. In this pleasure we experience and celebrate our dependence and our gratitude, for we are living from mystery, from creatures we did not make and powers we cannot comprehend."

Realizing the importance of the gift of food before us allows us to examine, as nutritionist Marc David writes, "How we eat is a reflection of how we live." Consuming food, like living our lives, can be done with extraneous chatter or with intention, consciously or unconsciously, hurriedly or not, fearfully or with courage. "And by eating with dignity, we learn to live with dignity."

Geoffrey Shugen Arnold, Sensei, brings the Buddhist perspective to the table as he demonstrates how, in the span of partaking of a meal, ritualized or not, we are realizing our entire existences. He poses the question: "There are lots of things to eat in this vast world. There's food, there's poison, there's the self, there's the Dharma. There's eating itself that can be eaten. How do we learn how to eat?" As Arnold traces the process of *oryoki*—the ritualized meal partaken at Buddhist retreats—he demonstrates that by eating with attention we can be freed from self-involvement to realize that we had everything we needed even before we sat down to eat.

This mystery of practicality and pleasure is manifested through a child's observations in the selection from writer and teacher Bich Minh Nguyen's memoir. Food becomes all kinds of sustenance—not just something that supports life, but also the condition of being supported. The author sees the spiritual in the food around her and how it links her to her physical and spiritual past and future.

Every bite we chew merits our attention. It's a quick prayer. A moment for meditation. An opportunity to pause and recognize our place in the food chain, to appreciate our great fortune at having food on our plates, to check in with ourselves and to savor our connection to the universe. It's remarkable that a mere omelet, a Brussels sprout, or a piece of candy corn holds so much power. Every morsel we consume gives us another opportunity to see the Sacred.

Karyn D. Kedar

THERE IS NOTHING MORE PROFOUND

There is nothing more profound than the breaking of
  bread.
God we ask Your blessing
For all who are hungry
And cannot come to eat.
Who do not know the feeling of a second helping,
Who know that the bread of affliction is real ...

Julia S. Kasdorf

ONION, FRUIT OF GRACE

Onion, fruit of grace,
you swell in the garden
hidden as the heart of God,
but you are not about religion.
Onion, frying into all those Os,
you are a perfect poet,
and you are not about that.
Onion, I love you,
you sleek, auburn beauty,
You break my heart though
I know you don't mean
to make me cry.

Peeling your paper skin,
I cry. Chopping you,
I cry. Slicing off
your wiry roots,
I cry like a penitent
at communion, onion.
Tasting grace, layer by layer,
I eat your sweet heart
that burns like the Savior's.
The sun crust you pull on
while you're still underground.

I've peeled it.
Onion, I'm eating
God's tears.

Wendell Berry

THE PLEASURES OF EATING

Many times, after I have finished a lecture on the decline of American farming and rural life, someone in the audience has asked, "What can city people do?"

"Eat responsibly," I have usually answered. Of course, I have tried to explain what I meant by that, but afterwards I have invariably felt that there was more to be said than I had been able to say. Now I would like to attempt a better explanation.

I begin with the proposition that eating is an agricultural act. Eating ends the annual drama of the food economy that begins with planting and birth. Most eaters, however, are no longer aware that this is true. They think of food as an agricultural product, perhaps, but they do not think of themselves as participants in agriculture. They think of themselves as "consumers." If they think beyond that, they recognize that they are passive consumers. They buy what they want—or what they have been persuaded to want—within the limits of wifery of the old household food economy. But one can be thus liberated only by entering a trap (unless one sees ignorance and helplessness as the signs of privilege, as many people apparently do). The trap is the ideal of industrialism: a walled city surrounded by valves that let merchandise in but no consciousness out. How does one escape this trap? Only voluntarily, the same way that one went in: by restoring one's consciousness of what is involved in eating; by reclaiming responsibility for one's own part in the food economy. One might begin with the illuminating principle of Sir Albert Howard's *The Soil and Health*, that we should understand "the whole problem of health in soil, plant, animal, and man as one great subject." Eaters, that is, must understand that eating takes place inescapably in the world, that it is inescapably an agricultural act, and that how we eat determines, to a considerable extent, how the world is used. This is a simple way of describing a relationship that is inexpressibly complex. To eat responsibly is to understand and enact, so far as one can, this complex relationship. What can one do? Here is a list, probably not definitive:

1. Participate in food production to the extent that you can. If you have a yard or even just a porch box or a pot in a sunny window, grow something to eat in it. Make a little compost of your kitchen scraps and use it for fertilizer. Only by growing some food for yourself can you become acquainted with the beautiful energy cycle that revolves from soil to seed to flower to fruit to food to offal to decay, and around again. You will be fully responsible for any food that you grow for yourself, and you will know all about it. You will appreciate it fully, having known it all its life.

2. Prepare your own food. This means reviving in your own mind and life the arts of kitchen and household. This should enable you to eat more cheaply, and it will give you a measure of "quality control": you will have some reliable knowledge of what has been added to the food you eat.

3. Learn the origins of the food you buy, and buy the food that is produced closest to your home. The idea that every locality should be, as much as possible, the source of its own food makes several kinds of sense. The locally produced food supply is the most secure, the freshest, and the easiest for local consumers to know about and to influence.

4. Whenever possible, deal directly with a local farmer, gardener, or orchardist. All the reasons listed for the previous suggestion apply here. In addition, by such dealing you eliminate the whole pack of merchants, transporters, processors, packagers, and advertisers who thrive at the expense of both producers and consumers.

5. Learn, in self-defense, as much as you can of the economy and technology of industrial food production. What is added to food that is not food, and what do you pay for these additions?

6. Learn what is involved in the best farming and gardening.

7. Learn as much as you can, by direct observation and experience if possible, of the life histories of the food species.

The last suggestion seems particularly important to me. Many people are now as much estranged from the lives of domestic plants and animals (except for flowers and dogs and cats) as they are from the lives of the wild ones. This is regrettable, for these domestic creatures are in diverse ways attractive; there is much pleasure in knowing them. And farming, animal husbandry, horticulture, and gardening, at their best, are complex and comely arts; there is much pleasure in knowing them, too.

It follows that there is great displeasure in knowing about a food economy that degrades and abuses those arts and those plants and animals and the soil from which they come. For anyone who does know something of the modern history of food, eating away from home can be a chore. My own inclination is to eat seafood instead of red meat or poultry when I am traveling. Though I am by no means a vegetarian, I dislike the thought that some animal has been made miserable in order to feed me. If I am going to eat meat, I want it to be from an animal that has lived a pleasant, uncrowded life outdoors, on bountiful pasture, with good water nearby and trees for shade. And I am getting almost as fussy about food plants. I like to eat vegetables and fruits that I know have lived happily and healthily in good soil, not the products of the huge, be-chemicaled factory-fields that I have seen, for example, in the Central Valley of California. The industrial farm is said to have been patterned on the factory production line. In practice, it looks more like a concentration camp.

The pleasure of eating should be an extensive pleasure, not that of the mere gourmet. People who know the garden in which their vegetables have grown and know that the garden is healthy will remember the beauty of the growing plants, perhaps in the dewy first light of morning when gardens are at their best. Such a memory involves itself with the food and is one of the pleasures of eating. The knowledge of the good health of the garden relieves and frees and comforts the eater. The same goes for eating meat. The thought of the good pasture and of the calf contentedly grazing flavors the steak. Some, I know, will think it bloodthirsty or worse to eat a fellow creature you have known all its life. On the contrary, I think it means that you eat with understanding and with gratitude. A significant part of the pleasure of eating is in one's accurate consciousness of the lives and the world from which food comes. The pleasure of eating, then, may be the best available standard of our health. And this pleasure, I think, is pretty fully available to the urban consumer who will make the necessary effort.

I mentioned earlier the politics, esthetics, and ethics of food. But to speak of the pleasure of eating is to go beyond those categories. Eating with the fullest pleasure—pleasure, that is, that does not depend on ignorance—is perhaps the profoundest enactment of our connection with the world. In this pleasure we experience and celebrate our dependence and our gratitude, for we are living from mystery, from creatures we did not make and powers we cannot comprehend. When I think of the meaning of food, I always remember these lines by the poet William Carlos Williams, which seem to me merely honest:

> *There is nothing to eat,*
> seek it where you will,
> but the body of the Lord.
> The blessed plants
> and the sea, yield it
> to the imagination
> intact.

Marc David

HOW WE EAT

What nourishes? What is it that truly feeds us and provides the satisfaction we seek? We believe that good nutrition nourishes us, and it does, yet it is easy to lose sight of all that nourishes and focus on nutrition alone. There is a wonderful scene in Woody Allen's movie *Sleeper* where he wakes up after two centuries of suspended animation. The scientists who have brought him out of this long sleep explain his plight, and one of the first questions he asks is, "Where are all my friends?" He is told that his friends are dead, to which he replies with his classic forlorn and quizzical look, "I don't understand it; they all ate organic rice."

The question of what nourishes is often difficult to answer because our dietary notions change constantly. What we thought was good to eat yesterday is not always what we think is good today.

Most nutritional assertions that originate from authoritative sources have a brief shelf life. Our nutritional information is not based on what is ultimately good to eat, but what we believe is good to eat at the time. Within this unstable state of affairs, one thing does remain constant—the connection between our relationship to food and our inner world. How we eat is a reflection of how we live. Our hurrying through life is reflected in hurrying through meals. Our fear of emotional emptiness is seen in our overeating. Our need for certainty and control is mirrored in strict dietary rules. Our looking for love in all the wrong places is symbolized in our use of food as a substitute for love.

The more we are aware of these connections, the greater the potential for our personal and inner satisfaction. For in changing the way we eat, we change the way we live. By focusing attention while eating, we learn to focus attention in any situation. By enjoying food, we begin to enjoy nourishment in all its forms. By loosening dietary restrictions, we learn to open up to life. By accepting our body as it is, we learn to love ourselves for who we are. And by eating with dignity, we learn to live with dignity.

Geoffrey Shugen Arnold, Sensei

JUST ENOUGH

Eating is something that every living creature can do without thinking, yet is there a way to eat *correctly?* There are so many things to consume in this vast world. There's food, there's poison, there's the self, there's the Dharma. There's eating itself that can be eaten. How can we eat so this very action is enlightened activity?

In Zen training, we study this through *oryoki*, the meal that we partake in during sesshins (silent Zen meditation intensives). In the Japanese word " *oryoki*," the character "o" means "equal to." "Ryo" means "amount," and "ki" is "container." *Oryoki* is the container that equals the appropriate amount. Some people's needs are great, others' are far less. Some eat far beyond their needs, others less than they should. Many people struggle with knowing how much to take. How can eating a bowl of rice become such a complicated affair?

Oryoki is a practice and a teaching of how to live. We begin *oryoki* by reviewing and chanting the four major events of the Buddha's life—his birth, enlightenment, teaching, and death.

> *Buddha was born at Kapilavastu, enlightened at Magadha,*
> *Taught at Paranasi, entered Nirvana at Kusinagara.*
> *Now I open Buddha Tathagata's eating bowls;*
> *May we be relieved from self-clinging with all sentient beings.*

Buddha was born ... The Buddha was born just like you and me, wet, wiggly, and screaming. Then he grew up, just like you and me, in his own time and place. In the course of his life there was a moment when he noticed that something wasn't quite right. Everything in his external world was fine, in fact, by most people's standards he was very privileged. Yet he couldn't shake a deep sense of dissatisfaction that grew within him, despite the luxury around him.

When we intone that he was enlightened at Magadha, contained within that simple statement is his own spiritual path after having left his home to seek the truth. He went through periods of great struggle as he meditated, struggled with feelings of desire and attachment, and faced his own mind. Then he came to realization, and after that he spent the rest of his life teaching. He lived a long time, and gave up the rest of his life simply to help others.

After his enlightenment, he could have had any kind of life he wanted. He chose to spend the rest of his life wandering and teaching, living the same life he asked his students to live. He begged, resolved conflicts within the Sangha, dealt with unruly disciples. There were challenges arising all the time, on all sorts of levels. He helped to resolve conflicts and prevent wars. And when there were wars he couldn't prevent, he just stood and witnessed the deep-seated stupidity and wasteful suffering. Just imagine the pain. And then he died, just like you and me.

Maezumi Roshi wrote that in those four lines beginning the meal there is the whole of *oryoki*. The verse seems like a brief history lesson, but it's asking us to reflect on where we come from and who before us has made it possible for us to be here right now. It's knowing what's required in order that we can open the Buddha's eating bowls.

"Now I open Buddha Tathagata's eating bowls." What's the "now"? Now—at this particular moment in time? Now—because the Buddha was born, enlightened, taught, and died? Is it because of this that we are actually able to open those bowls? For most of us, before we've even finished chanting these lines, already there's self-clinging, attachment, and desire....

We chant, "May we be relieved from self-clinging," and it is a relief. To be free from self-clinging is the greatest relief of all. Frequently, people ask how they can get to the point where they can let go of something they're attached to. The easiest route is to feel the full weight of the burden of not letting go. That's the straight ticket. You can try to talk yourself into letting go. You can find support in the teachings. You can get encouragement from a teacher or be inspired by others around you. But when you feel the strain of your own effort of clinging, then you understand as never before that it's time to lay the burden down.

After unwrapping our bowls, we say, *In the midst of the Three Treasures, with all sentient beings, let us recite the names of Buddha.* Let's look at the first line, "In the midst of the Three Treasures." When you have taken refuge in the Three Treasures—the Buddha, Dharma, and Sangha—and are stuck on something (or stuck outside of something), you know that you have everything you need to relieve yourself of your burden. Another way of saying this is that you *only* have at your disposal what you need to relieve yourself of that burden. In both cases, there's nowhere outside of yourself to go and there's nothing you lack. You can turn to the wisdom of the enlightened mind within your teacher and within yourself. You can rely upon the teachings and practices of the Buddha. You can trust in the good company and fine example of the Sangha, the practitioners of the Buddha's dharma.

Trungpa Rinpoche has an illustrative analogy for this situation. Imagine you're washed up on a desert island. If you're going to stay alive—and thrive—you'll need to do so on that very island, there's nowhere else you can go. If you're committed to living this life, then whatever you need is going to be found on that island. Otherwise, you're out of luck. What then happens to the one on the island? You get busy, seeing what's there and what you can use. Learning how to use it and putting it to work. If we do have alternatives, we'll tend to wait, or turn away from ourselves and the true source of the problem as well as the gate of our liberation. Taking refuge in the Three Treasures is a recognition that there is no ship coming to save us, ever.

And then we start the rest of the chant, "Seventy-two labors brought us this food; we should know how it comes to us." How did it get here, into this bowl? Did you notice that a server actually got down on his or her knees, eye-to-eye with you, and served the food into your bowl? Knowing how the food comes to us is the same as knowing how to receive it. Are we talking about the rice in the bowl or are we talking about any kind of sustenance? How did this moment come to us?

One of the greatest misunderstandings of our times, especially in our culture, is to conclude that because we hand some money across the counter when we are purchasing something, that we have completed the transaction, and we have been relieved of our burden of debt. The further away we get from recognizing the multitude of actions required to bring us a piece of fruit, a computer, or a car, an education, public transportation, or any of the innumerable things we count on every day, the easier it is to think that by paying some amount of money we have fulfilled our responsibility for living on this planet and consuming life.

Recently I read about the World Trade Organization [WTO] meetings in Cancun during which a Korean farmer committed suicide protesting the globalized trade practices of the WTO. It was impossible for him to sustain his life any longer as a farmer. Imagine how desperate a farmer must be to take his own life over policies created by people he has never seen and who know nothing of the realities of his life. Do we know how the food comes to us? It's not always a pretty picture. It's not an easy problem to solve. But we should know. At least, we should start there and be responsible for knowing just that much.

To get here, we have to want to know. That's why the verse is asking if we know how it comes to us. Because we have to want to know. Otherwise we can so easily assume that this food simply came from the kitchen downstairs or the store on the corner. We will conclude that it didn't come from anywhere that has to do with human lives and the health of the planet. We'll decide without knowing that it's really not important where it came from.

As we receive this offering [of this food], we should consider whether our virtue and practice deserve it. This is not a matter of being worthy or unworthy. Everyone is welcome to sit down to the meal, but are we deserving? Should we be deserving simply because we're here and we need the food? This teaching is pointing to the interdependent nature of all things. In receiving there must be giving. We are always receiving and always giving, but what are we offering? If we're mired in our greed, fear and anger, and ignorance, then it will be very difficult to offer something that is not arising from those states of mind. This line challenges us to consider—to be aware of—what we are creating moment after moment.

As we desire the natural order of mind to be free from clinging, we must be free from greed. If we don't want to be giving greed and anger, then we must return to our natural order of mind. "Natural" here means without contrivance or manipulation, that is, without self-clinging. And in order to be free from clinging, we have to be free from greed. That makes good sense. We can see that at the very heart of clinging is greed.

Wendell Berry talks about our greed this way:

We've lived by the assumption that what was good for us would be good for the world. We've been wrong. We must change our lives so that it will be possible to live by the contrary assumption that what is good for the world will be good for us. That requires that we make the effort to know the world and learn what is good for it. We must learn to cooperate in its processes and to yield to its limits. But even more important, we must learn to acknowledge that the creation is full of mystery. We will never clearly understand it. We must abandon arrogance and stand in awe. We must recover the sense of the majesty of the creation and the ability to be worshipful in its presence. For it is only on the condition of humility and reverence before the world that our species will be able to remain in it.

Berry says this attitude of self-centeredness—and thus seeing the world and all its creatures from our own self-centered perspective—is not sustainable. We have to understand what the world wants and needs. I have to understand what you want and need in totality. When we are free from greed, your well-being and happiness become my need, my well-being. This is the Buddhist sense of compassion, of living in harmony with all beings, animate and inanimate. When we begin to sincerely inquire into life, we begin to understand that we will never understand all of it. Awe and humility arise out of that and in that humility is respect for that which we will never know, and for that which sustains us. Because of it we are here, and yet we can't fully know it. Yet we can serve, we can offer ourselves freely. This is not a matter of knowing. Rather, when we go beyond the thinking mind tethered to the sense of a separate self, there is no bondage and thus, there is giving freely. In giving freely there is then receiving freely, without hindrance; receiving in perfect accord with everything.

Bich Minh Nguyen

THE PLUM'S EYE

One late afternoon when [my grandmother] Noi was out watering the garden, I slipped into her room. The day had gotten sticky with humidity, and the brightness of the outdoors made everything inside feel cooler and dim. I could tell it was going to be one of those nights when my siblings and I would sleep in the basement to stay cool. I didn't know where everyone was to make the house so empty: Vinh probably playing Transformers somewhere with [my neighbor] Jennifer's brother; Anh hanging out at a friend's house; Crissy with her friends, maybe smoking in the parking lot behind Ken-O-Sha; my uncles at their jobs; my father at North American Feather; Rosa working downtown at the Hispanic Institute. For once, I was practically alone in the house.

As I studied the altar, I realized that fruit was all Buddha had to eat. Except for holidays it was the same thing day in and day out— lunch was dinner, dinner was breakfast. My father had tried to explain that Buddha believed in simplicity and having as few things as possible. So I guessed that he was okay with just fruit—maybe he even preferred it. I couldn't comprehend that. Looking up at Buddha I wanted to ask, *that's all?* I didn't know what it was not to want. For I could hardly name all the different meals I wished to have. Dinners of sirloin tips and Shake 'n Bake, Beef Stroganoff and shepherd's pie. Jeno's pizzas and thermoses of SpaghettiOs. Great squares of Jell-O bouncing through the air as they did in the commercials; Bundt cakes; chocolate parfaits; rounds of crusty lattice-topped pies. I wanted all the dinners from *Little House on the Prairie*, all those biscuits and salt pork, grease seeping into fried potatoes. I wanted every packaged and frozen dinner from the grocery store; Noodle Roni, Hamburger Helper Hungry Man, Stouffer's, Swanson, and Banquet. All the trays with separate compartments for Salisbury steak, whipped potatoes, and peas. I wanted to take it all, hoard it, hide it away. If I were a spirit, I would fill myself with meals culled from the city around me. People in their pretty houses would sit down to dinners of nothing. They would take their eyes off their plates for just one second and the food would be gone. They would open their refrigerators; empty. Their pantries would be cleaned out. Cupboards bare, the doors swinging open to emphasize the blank space. I would take from restaurants; Brann's, Big Boy, Charley's Crab—all the white American meals I longed to try. If I were a spirit, I would eat more than enough to get me through the night.

Noi had closed the shades to keep the sun out. The room smelled of her favorite sandalwood incense. I sat on the bed for a moment, listening to the quiet of the house. The heat pressed on me and I shut my eyes, trying to meditate. But I could think of nothing but the altar. The burnished statue of Buddha rose above me. His always closed eyes, his gown of glimmering folds. He was nothing like the fat, happy Buddha statue we had in the basement. That Buddha, dyed a festive red, had an open mouth and eyes squished up in laughter. He sat with one knee raised, showing off his potbelly, not at all resembling this smooth Buddha with his face of radiant calm.

I leaned in close to the altar to sniff the wood and incense. I took in the gazes of my grandfather and uncle and great-grandmother. How far these pictures had traveled to come back to us. My father had said the spirits of our ancestors could find us anywhere. In between their photographs two wrought-iron trays held plums, nectarines, and bananas in near-pyramids of offering and respect. An afternoon snack for my ancestors, a dinner for Buddha.

With one fingertip I touched the stem of a plum, whose violet skin always looked dusty. For just a moment, I hovered over Buddha.

His eyes were still closed. Sometimes, when we wanted to scare each other, Anh and I talked about how one day Buddha's eyes would fly open, shooting out beams of light. I waited a minute longer, until I heard the sound of the basement door opening and sliding shut. Then I ran out of the room, pushing the plum into my shorts pocket as I hurried out the front door.

I crossed our yard to the Vander Wal's—Jennifer must have been at vacation Bible school—and shimmied up their plum tree. How many times had Jennifer and I sat up here among the leaves, dreaming up one of our clubs? In the full bloom of summer the leaf-thick limbs took us in and kept us hidden. I settled into my usual spot, where two sturdy branches seemed to create a lounge chair just right for my size. I pulled Buddha's plum from my pocket and examined it as I had when my sister and I were little, marveling at the mystery of the fruit. I looked for some answer in its skin but found nothing. The guilt I felt was the same as shame. I knew that this was where the test would end—me in the tree with the stolen plum. My father had said that Buddha had given up all possessions of his royal birth and become enlightened. Buddha never claimed to be a god. He could not be tested. He had no wrath. He granted no miracles or wishes. He asked me to prove nothing ...

... I bit into the plum. I was struck by the contrast of the yellow flesh, limned with the scarlet underside of the skin. I took small bites so as not to waste a drop of juice. Too soon, the fruit was gone and the pit lay in my palm. It was an eye, I realized. A wrinkled, wizened eye. I thought about how the spirits were always watching out for us. They were never too far away. I set the eye on a branch where I could face it, and it me. I sat there for a long time. I heard the sound of Linda Vander Wal's car leaving and then returning, brining Jennifer back from Bible school. I listened to the car doors slam and the murmur of their voices, the screen door shutting them into their house. The daylight began to glow—that quiescent hour before the beginning of sunset—and I knew it was time to go home. I left the plum's eye in the plum tree. It was gone the next time I climbed up there. I imagined it carried off by the wind, or by my ancestor's spirits, coming to collect the meager offering I had left behind.

Give food to the

Hungry, O Lord,

And hunger

For You to those who have food.

CHRISTIAN GRACE

 Part Six

FASTS

LETTING GO

ood and the absence of food, emptiness and fullness, there's no separation. Without one, you can't have the other. Sometimes, discovering what is sacred about food is best accomplished by intentionally abstaining from it. There are occasions when the absence of food can reveal much of what food represents—our cravings, the promise of living another day, unity, and the things we take for granted. Doing without food can forge a deeper empathy for people who are hungry. Fasting can also point out a spiritual hunger—the waves of want within our own souls.

Writer Omid Safi recalls the fasting and feasting of the Ramadans of his childhood and compares them to his realizations as an adult. For Safi, Ramadan became a way to feel the "pain and suffering" for those who live with basic physical hunger. As Safi grew older and had children of his own, his understanding of fasting expanded to encompass all the sufferings of others, a way to feel all "the pain of others" and a means to "have the courage to bring some healing into this fractured world."

Rabbi Irwin Kula and writer Vanessa L. Ochs echo Safi's considerations as they explain that fasting is more than "a cruel test." In this passage, fasting is seen to be a means of building community and "admitting our frailty." They conclude the meditation with a quote from the biblical prophet Isaiah that directly links fasting to the holy for as we "break every yoke ... a cleansing light shall break forth like the dawn."

Emptying himself of his very human drive to accomplish and conquer, spiritual teacher Ram Dass shows how fasting is about the mind as much as the body. It's easy to gorge on our own egos. Although it's all very well and good to renounce food and perceive oneself as holy, not until one renounces *hunger* can fasting truly release us from our egos and offer a connection with the physical and spiritual yearnings of our fellow human beings: "It's release, not self-denial."

Scott Nearing's self-starvation nourished him spiritually. For him, fasting wasn't as much about hastening his demise or testing his will as it was about accepting the end and moving from life with dignity. Author Helen Nearing writes of her husband's powerful "methodical and conscious choice" to abstain from food as he moved toward death "into the invisible." Through fasting he willingly let go of his corporeal body and "deliberately and purposefully chose the time and the way of his leaving." By abstaining from food, Scott let go of the tangible, meaningless ties that can serve to bind us to a place that is as transient as our very lives.

A koanlike excerpt from the eighth century attributed to Rabi'a al-'Adawiyya, one of the central female figures in the Sufi tradition, offers a teaching paradox that shows us that our relationship transcends the physical nature of the food itself and speaks to our relationship to God or what we perceive as holy. There's a lot about choice here, as well as about the connection between faith, freedom, and food.

Acknowledging choice is a thread writer Jessica Swift picks up and weaves into her essay, "I Can Eat Chocolate for Breakfast." She encourages awareness of our universal connections as she asks, "Just as I am compelled to fill my own belly, I must also ache with the same burning emptiness hunger ignites ... for until none of us are hungry, aren't we all?"

By abstaining from food, we can create a space within ourselves (quite literally) that can free us to connect to the Divine. Just as one should take physical cautions, one should take spiritual precautions before fasting as well, for as Ram Dass writes, "I've come to recognize that the real *tapasya* [renunciation] happens when we are so ripe to do it that we just *do* it. We do it joyfully, with a feeling of 'Yeah—of course. That's what happens now.' We do it with a feeling of 'Whew! Now I can be rid of that one.' It's release, not self-denial." Ramana Maharshi said, "I didn't eat, and they said I was fasting." Right there in that statement is the essence of *tapasya*. As long as we *think* we're doing the austerity—'look at me! I'm giving this up!'—it's just another ego trip. Whatever we may think we're renouncing, we're just stuffing our egos with both hands."

Omid Safi

RAMADAN, DATE OMELETS, AND GLOBAL COMPASSION

Ramadan was simpler in my childhood: It was about date omelets.

We got up around 4 or 4:30 a.m. to have a *suhur*, also called *sahari*, meaning a dawn-time meal. After that, no food and no water until sunset time. For the grown-ups, it meant no smoking, and as they love to joke about it, no sex until sunset. Then we would break our fasts with a meal called *iftar*. Getting out of bed was always a titanic struggle, but not on Ramadan mornings. We got to have a special treat on those days: date omelets.

My mom, God bless her precious heart, would get up at 4 in the Ramadan morning and cook *sahari* for us. We got to have date omelets, which must have at least eight thousand calories. She would take four or five fresh dates, cook them in some butter (no margarine, please), and then mix it with some scrambled eggs. Sugar, fat, protein. Oh, and a tall glass of chocolate milk, and another glass of water. Happiness on a table, served up at 4:30 a.m. We lived for that meal. We were not allowed to have date omelets at any other time of the year, no matter how much we begged for it.

Kids are not required to fast for the month of Ramadan. (Neither are the elderly, the sick, those who are traveling, women who are nursing or pregnant, etc.) As children, we didn't have to fast, and yet it was an important rite of passage to wake up with our family.

Ramadan was, and continues to be, a more spiritual time around our households. People are a bit more considerate, a bit more mindful.

Fewer arguments over the TV remote. Even my family members who did not do the regular five-times-a-day prayers fasted. To not fast would be ... rude. Ramadan is about food, and it is about more than food. It is about cleansing one's heart and soul. People watch what they say, what they listen to, what they look at. The words were spoken with a bit more compassion, and folks ended arguments before they began by reminding each other that it was Ramadan.

My father used to tell us that fasting was a privilege. He said that we chose to not eat from sunup to sundown, whereas there are people in the world for whom not eating lunch or snacks was a daily fact of life. In being hungry, we are to feel their pain and suffering. He would often repeat this Persian poem by Sa'di:

> The Children of Adam are members of one body,
> made from the same source.
> If one feels pain,
> the others can not be indifferent to it.
> If you are unmoved by the suffering of others,
> you are not worthy of the name human being.
>   (Sa'di, The Rose Garden)

One of the common customs in the Muslim world is to take food to those in need in Ramadan. There is often no central collecting agency to do this. The challenge was to do this without in any way reducing the dignity of those who were presented with the food. Charity personalized, dignity un-compromised. That was the goal.

I am thinking about Ramadan a lot these days as well. Missing those date omelets. And missing what felt like the simplicity of the times. They were not simple days, of course, as it was the time immediately preceding the Iranian Revolution of 1979. But to my eyes they seemed like simple days.

Ramadan is hard these days. Not eating food is the easy part. Ramadan is in winter these days, which means the fast can last less than 10 hours or so, depending on what part of the country you live in. It was often as long as 16 hours when Ramadan was in summer.

The hard part is feeling the suffering of others. I am a parent now. Before I am a Muslim, I am a parent. Before I am an American, I am a parent. And this Ramadan I am thinking a lot about children.

I think about the children whose parents never came home from the World Trade Center and the Pentagon. The children whose parents were on the four planes on September 11, and the ones whose parents were on the American Airlines plane that went down November 12. Even now as I look at my son and daughter watching *Arthur* on PBS, tears swell up in my eyes as I think about those children whose Ramadan, Hanukkah, and Christmas this year will be spent without their parents.

All of our children are precious, the ones here, the ones there, the ones everywhere. I have children now, which means my life is no longer my own. I have an eight-year-old son, and this Ramadan I will offer him date omelets at dawn time. And I will hug him tight— nappy hair, sleepy eyes, nasty breath, and all. May he grow up to be one who feels the pain of others as his own. May he have the courage to bring some healing into this fractured world.

And may he like date omelets ...

Rabbi Irwin Kula and Vanessa L. Ochs

A MEDITATION ON FASTING

Fasting might seem like a cruel test to see if we can deny our bodies food. Yet, at the heart of this practice is a desire to shift our attention away from the body's immediate needs and to focus on spiritual concerns. The logic goes something like this: when we fast, we are faced with admitting our frailty. In that weakened state we examine the parts of ourselves that are fragile and strengthen them with meditations and supplications. Fasting together as a community, we examine our failings and resolve to strengthen one another in the weeks to come....

Why, when we fasted, did You not see? ... This is My chosen fast: to loosen all the bonds that bind people unfairly, to let the oppressed go free, to break every yoke. Share your bread with the hungry, shelter the homeless, clothe the naked, and turn toward those in need. Then a cleansing light shall break forth like the dawn ... then you shall call and the Lord will answer (adapted from Isaiah 58).

Ram Dass

STUFFING OUR EGOS

Fasting was an interesting one for me, because I have always had an intense relationship with food. I learned from my mother to equate food with love, so by the time I was ten I was wearing pants in size double Z, with balloon seats. I was definitely *deep* into the oral trip.

Then it was 1967, and I was at the temple in India. I noticed that everybody there fasted a lot, so one day I said to my teacher, "Hari Dass, can I fast?" (Actually, I didn't *say* it—I *wrote* it on the slate I carried because we were *maun*, silent, at that time.) Hari Dass answered, "If you'd like." I asked, "How long should I fast for?" He said, "Four days would be good." So I asked him, "How long do *you* fast?" He wrote, "Nine days, on every new moon." I thought, "Well, if he can do it, I can do it." So I wrote, "I will fast for nine days." And I looked very holy.

The time came, and I started the fast. And I then proceeded to spend the entire nine days thinking about nothing but food. I thought about the Thanksgiving dinners I'd had as a child; I visualized the roast turkey, and the sweet potatoes with the little marshmallows on top, and the different kinds of stuffing, and how the gravy would smell, and what the first bite would taste like—I lived that out again and again and again. I thought about all the different restaurants I'd been to around the United States, about the cracked crab in the Northwest, and the steak at Original Joe's, in San Francisco, and the bouillabaisse in New Orleans, and the Lobster Savannah in Boston and—oh, boy! I'd been a cross between a gourmet and a gourmand for years, so I had a rich stock of memories to draw on.

I did complete the fast. I made it through all nine days. But the interesting question was, while I was so busy fasting, what was it I was feeding?

Three months later, when I did my next nine-day fast, I was getting much better. ("Better"—a new ego trip!) Now I spent the whole time thinking only about foods I could eat as a yogi. So I thought about spinach with lemon on it, and steaming bowls of rice, and fresh hot chapattis, and milk. I was doing all these fasts, thinking, "Aren't I good? I'm doing nine-day fasts, just like the book says. I'm becoming a great hatha yogi." And yet there were very few waking hours when I was not obsessing about food.

Time passed, and then a few years afterward, I was back in India again. Some friends and I were staying in a little village, and it seemed like a good opportunity to do another long fast. But this time, except for the fact that at noon, lemon and water or ginger tea was brought instead of food, I never even noticed I was fasting. I was just busy doing other things instead of eating. About halfway through, I thought, "Oh, *this* is what fasting is about. Far out!" It's not about renouncing food— it's about renouncing hunger! I hadn't even known what it was all *about* before, because I was so busy thinking that the ego-tripping I was doing was *tapasya*, that it was an austerity of some sort.

I've come to recognize that the real *tapasya* happens when we are so ripe to do it that we just *do* it. We do it joyfully, with a feeling of "Yeah—of course. That's what happens now." We do it with a feeling of "Whew! Now I can be rid of that one." It's release, not self-denial. Ramana Maharshi said, "I didn't eat, and they said I was fasting." Right there in that statement is the essence of *tapasya*. As long as we think *we're* doing the austerity—"look at me! I'm giving this up!"— it's just another ego trip. Whatever we may think we're renouncing, we're just stuffing our egos with both hands.

Helen Nearing

CASTING OFF HIS BODY

For a long time [my husband] Scott and I had both been interested in the subject of life after death. We had an intellectual curiosity about dying, great expectations of what it would be like, and now that Scott was coming closer to the end of his life we devoted much time to talking and reading about the subject. There were dozens of books on death and dying in our library, some of which (notably a rare three-volume set, *Before Death, At Death,* and *After Death* by the French astronomer Camille Flammarion) had belonged to my father years ago.

We believed in the continuity of life and continuance of consciousness in some form. We were eager for more encounters that we believed awaited us, more opportunities. Death, we felt, was a transition, not a termination. It was an exit-entrance between two areas of life.

In answer to a question on the subject from an old agnostic friend, Roger Baldwin, Scott wrote: "By many people death is considered an end. For others of us, death is a change; a good deal like the change from day to night—always thus far followed by another day. Never the same twice, but a procession of days.

"The human body turns into dust when the life force is withdrawn, only to be replaced by other forms that the life force assumes. The change, called death, is terminal for our bodies but not for higher expressions of the same life forces.

"I believe there is a revival, or survival, in some form. Our life goes on."

Scott had long talked of a purposeful and deliberate death. He was not going to wait until he was totally incapacitated and had become a burden to himself and others. He did not want to go through the horrors of a long decay in a nursing home.

"Why do we make such a hullabaloo of our last days and of dying?" he queried. Instead of quiet harmonious fading away in congenial familiar surroundings, we ship our loved ones to hospitals and nursing homes, where at great expense, they are maintained by strangers who try to stave off death by artificial means instead of easing and abetting the process. We enter with discomfort and a cry, but we can depart in dignity and completion, having fulfilled at least in part our purpose...."

... A month and a half before Scott went, a month before his hundredth birthday, while sitting with a group at the table one day, he said: "I think I won't eat anymore." He never took solid food again. He deliberately and purposefully chose the time and the way of his leaving. It was to be methodical and conscious. He would cast off his body by fasting.

Death by fasting is not a violent form of suicide; it is a slow gentle diminution of energies, a peaceful way to leave, voluntarily. Externally and internally he was prepared. He had always liked Robert Louis Stevenson's "Glad did I live and gladly die, and I lay me down with a will." Now he could put this into practice. He himself inaugurated his own technique for dying: let the body itself give up life.

I acquiesced, realizing how animals often leave life—creeping away out of sight and denying themselves food. For a month I fed Scott just on juices when he wanted any liquids: apple, orange, banana, grape, whatever he could swallow. Then he said: "I would like only water." Yet he did not sicken. He was still lucid and spoke with me, but his body was extremely emaciated. The life force in him was lessening.

A week more on water, and he was completely detached from life, ready to slip easily into that good night. His body had dried up; now it was withering away, and he could tranquilly and peacefully retire from it. I was with him on his couch and quietly urged him on, the morning of August 24, 1983.

Half aloud, I intoned an old Native American chant: "Walk tall as the trees; live strong as the mountains; be gentle as the spring winds; keep warmth of summer in your heart, and the Great Spirit will always be with you."

"You don't have to hold on to anything, my love," I murmured to him. "Just let go of the body. Go with the tide. Flow with it. You have lived a fine life. You have done your bit. Enter into a new life. Go into the light. Love goes with you. Everything here is all right."

Slowly, gradually, he detached himself, breathing less and less, fainter and fainter; then he was off and free, like a dry leaf from the tree, floating down and away. "All ... right" [*sic*], he breathed, seeming to testify to the all-rightness of everything, and was gone. I felt the visible pass into the invisible.

Rabi'a al-'Adawiyya

MIRACLE ONION

One day Rabi'a and her serving-girl were getting ready to break a fast of several days. The serving-girl needed an onion and was about to go next door and borrow one, but Rabi'a said: "Forty years ago I vowed never to ask for anything from anyone but God—we can do without onions."

Just then a bird flew over, and dropped an onion into Rabi'a's frying pan, peeled and ready to fry.

"Interesting but not convincing," she said. "Am I supposed to believe that God is an onion-vender? I mean, really."

That day they fried their bread without onions.

Jessica Swift

I CAN EAT CHOCOLATE
FOR BREAKFAST

I can eat chocolate for breakfast, or not. Having this choice speaks to the power I, as an individual, possess. A power many have never—and will never—experience. In my hunger I see a simple need that must be, and easily can be, met. I can fulfill this need time and time again and exercise my personal power of choice while satisfying a seemingly endless appetite. Yet why is my choice so powerful? Because I have it and can use it. I can eat, or not. Feel hungry, or not. I can choose what I eat. I can choose how to eat.

Not so far away are many people so unlike me, and yet we are the same. Our hearts beat, we inhale, exhale. Our eyes water with cleansing tears when they are dry or when our beating hearts swell with a tide of sadness that can only escape through the portals to our souls. Yet they have no choice about their hunger—how to end it, how to sate the very physical need, what to do for the eternal stretch of empty tomorrows until there are no more. In this we will never be the same.

If I eat chocolate for breakfast it is not enough to simply wave a hand in acknowledgment of the "them" who are without—that "them" is me, but not. Just as I am compelled to fill my own belly, I must also ache with the same burning emptiness hunger ignites. I must act in a way that sustains me physically, and revel in the beauty and wonder and blessing and divine gift that is food. Then I must daily decide to choose to end our hunger—for until none of us are hungry, aren't we all?

Care less for the harvest

than how it is shared,

and your life will have meaning

and your heart will have peace.

KENT NERBURN

Part Seven

FEASTS

REAPING

You're going to reap just what you sow.

LOU REED

So many feasts are celebrations of the breaking of fasts—thanksgivings expressed in various faiths. Be it a physical or a spiritual craving, it's hard to appreciate the gift of plenty if you haven't been genuinely empty first. Feasts are the flip side of fasting—through sharing our bounty, celebration, and preparing and consuming special and sometimes religiously significant foods, we chart yet another path to the Sacred—allowing the feast to fill us up with the Divine.

Feasts require community—they never happen in isolation. Feasts imply company, family, people other than our selves. This is well illustrated by Rabbi Rami Shapiro's description of heaven and hell where, "The only rule is this: you must use the utensils provided, each being six feet in length. Those who attempt to feed themselves with these tools starve, for they cannot maneuver the tools to reach their own mouths. Those who learn to feed others are themselves fed in turn."

Connection to community and heritage unifies two selections written by women who relate to their cultural and spiritual traditions, as well as their families, through food. For author Diana Abu-Jaber it's steam-lamp-soggy Middle Eastern cooking in a college cafeteria that ends her fast of separation from family and friends. She writes, "And while it's cold and overcooked, I still taste fried chickpeas, the golden, mellow fundament of falafel, and, embedded deeper within, the sun-soaked air of Jordan. The taste is clear and direct as emotion, glowing inside me, keenly edged with longing—a wallop of a feeling. Reassured, I look up and say, 'I've heard angels at dinner.'"

Lynne Meredith Schreiber links memories of past feasts to the future of her Jewish faith as she discovers that celebration, "That gift of family, of knowing who I am in a context of people, is priceless."

Writer and poet Mary Rose O'Reilley doesn't hesitate to tie food to the Sacred. Although the feast she envisions in "Key Lime Pie" is a bit more fantastical, O'Reilley evokes renewal, wonder, and transcendence of the logical to reach the Sublime to be reborn in the moment.

A feast doesn't have to be lavish. Sometimes it's as simple as raisins in oatmeal. Through her recollection of her days as a novice nun, Sister Joan Chittister, OSB, reminds us, "the celebration of life has something to do with food. Food is the glue and the center of human community making."

What you put into the universe comes back to you and then some. The seed planted with trust in the spring, an act of kindness, a prayer of supplication or gratitude, or raisins in oatmeal all help us recognize that every time we encounter food, from a bowl of rice to a wedding buffet, it's a chance to join with one person or thousands and experience our bounty as a manifestation of the Sacred.

Rabbi Rami Shapiro

HEAVEN AND HELL

Heaven and hell are a single feast, with everyone seated at a grand table overflowing with the finest food and drink. The only rule is this: you must use the utensils provided, each being six feet in length. Those who attempt to feed themselves with these tools starve, for they cannot maneuver the tools to reach their own mouths. Those who learn to feed others are themselves fed in turn. The first are in hell, the second in heaven, but the feast is common to them both.

Diana Abu-Jaber

I'VE HEARD ANGELS AT DINNER

Barely a month into the semester, the mornings are charged with sharp, clean filaments of winter air. By October, I can look out of my eighth-floor window and view the campus grounds all the way to the start of Lake Ontario glowing in a crystal ice sheet. Light snow glitters in the air. For some reason, I miss my childhood. It's a subtler, more ancient form of homesickness that I find absorbing, a delicious sadness.

In late October, Hillel, the Jewish student organization, papers the hallways with posters for a Jewish Foods Day as well as a menu that includes a number of the foods I grew up with. The poster features the Middle Eastern dishes that I think of as the Trinity: falafel, hummus, and baba ghanouj. I study the sign and recall Aunt Aya's teachings on the origins of dishes. Does falafel belong to a nation? A culture? I stand in the corridor, hands on my hips, mulling over the poster.

Whatever the nationality or religion, I'm excited about this event. I've never heard of anyone outside of our family serving such dishes—especially falafel, which is a messy, deep-fried affair. Better to leave falafel sandwiches to the guys with full-body aprons selling it from carts.

I try to convince a number of my dormmates [*sic*] to attend Jewish Foods Day with me. But the girls in my all-girls dorm are turning out to be finicky, hothouse flowers. They spend hours lined up in the mirror-lined bathrooms, blow-drying their hair to glassy straightness, painting their toenails, or lolling in bed eating ice cream and pizza. In the end, I manage to entice only Elise, who happens to be Jewish, and to harangue my two roommates into submission. Annie is a stolid, good-natured Irish-Catholic girl from working-class Long Island. She owns two pairs of jeans and six T-shirts and wears her long brown hair parted cleanly down the middle so that it hangs in two shanks on her shoulders. Courtney is a strawberry-blonde Southern debutante with sticky mascaraed lashes. She is engaged to the former captain of her high school football team. "I don't like anything new, pretty much ever," she says in her buttery accent. But, grudgingly, they agree to go.

We travel together in a clutch to the cafeteria in the student union building, where Hillel has set up a small assemblage of caterer's chafing dishes and orange heat lamps against one wall. Besides the falafel, hummus, and baba ghanouj, there's an okra stew and a plate of sinewy chunks of beef that they're calling *shawerma*. Alongside all of this is a tub full of three-bean salad. We join the sparse crowd, sliding trays through the line. Exuberant student workers with shining dark eyes mill around greeting everyone individually with a handshake and a bright "Shalom!" But two older men standing glumly behind the tubs and dishing out the food are muttering in Arabic, discussing the three-bean salad:

"I can't explain it."

"But what is it? I didn't bring it."

"I think it must be Jewish food."

"But where did it come from?"

"The Super Duper Market."

After we settle at our table, Courtney, her eyes continuously damp from her contacts, looks around and whispers, "Is everyone around here really Jewish?"

"Courtney, half the kids at this school are Jewish," Annie says.

"They are?"

"And Diana's Arabic!"

Courtney stares at me as if I've been hiding something.

Elise examines her plate of food, then finally samples some cucumber salad; she praises it lavishly and encourages the rest of us to dive in. Annie, pleased by the break from the dining hall fare, says the hummus reminds her of peanut butter and scoops her pita bread through the dip in wide streaks, then goes back for more. Courtney daintily pokes at the falafel, rolling it around without managing to break the fried crust, and I have to resist the urge to slap her hand. She refuses to touch her food with anything but metal utensils.

The truth is that the food on our trays looks lumpen and uninspiring. It's been steamed to death under the heat lamps. The hummus is dull as clay, the baba ghanouj thick and bitter. The dried-out falafel crumbles on impact with the bread, and there isn't any tahini sauce or chopped tabbouleh to spruce things up. Even the three-bean salad releases a viscous mucilaginous fluid that I scrape to the edge of my plate. I feel too disappointed to eat more than a bite or two.

"Well, really, Diana," Courtney says, "I don't know what you expect me to do with this Jewish food. I'm not even Jewish."

I grind my molars together and stab a cucumber slice. I glance at the two gloomy Arab men behind the chafing dishes and lower my eyes, irrationally worried that they might somehow know me.

Now Courtney looks thoughtful. "They should have an Episcopalian food week, too. I wonder if they'd ever do that here?"

Elise snorts. "Oh, and what would that be, Courtney? Sugar peeps?" Courtney is renowned in the dorm for subsisting on marshmallow chicks.

"I'm just saying, I don't see the point of getting all high and mighty about food anyway," she says, her voice singed with hurt. "I mean, since when is food religious? It's not like it can make you hear angels or something."

Elise and I are both looking at her. Elise takes a big bite of falafel and says, "I feel sorry for you."

Suddenly reinvigorated, I scoop up one of the hard little falafels in a corner of pita and take a bite, expecting it will taste as bad as it looks. And while it's cold and overcooked, I still taste fried chickpeas, the golden, mellow fundament of falafel, and, embedded deeper within, the sun-soaked air of Jordan. The taste is clear and direct as emotion, glowing inside me, keenly edged with longing—a wallop of a feeling. Reassured, I look up and say, "I've heard angels at dinner."

"Does this taste like angels to you?" Annie asks me grinning.

"Y'all are like religious fanatics," Courtney says with a fastidious sniff. She puts down her fork and knife. "And I'm not hungry."

Lynne Meredith Schreiber

INHERITING THE EARTH

"Grandpa always made the salad," I say in the dark of my five-year-old son's room. "He chopped cucumbers and tomatoes very small and diced hard-boiled eggs to throw on top." Asher scrunches his nose; he doesn't like eggs.

Grandma's veal scallopine was made of thin slices of veal in bubbling tomato sauce. When I ate there on Friday nights as a child, Grandpa raced through the prayer over wine, sending me, my sister and grandmother into fits of giggles. Grandpa was Weeble-like with a hawk-like nose, but he laughed heartily and his hands were satin-soft. Even in my twenties, I held his hand, the wide square smooth nails, freckles from age and sun dotting his warm skin, holding on, both of us, as if for balance.

"Tell what you had for dessert," Asher urges. When I say, "Fudgsicles," he leans back on the pillow, arms behind his head. It's as if we ate gold.

Friday nights at my grandparents' house were lit by flickering candlelight and the low rumble of Hebrew prayers. They were the only people in my family to celebrate the Sabbath. Saturday mornings, I trailed after my grandfather's long wool tallit prayer shawl at services, sitting amid the hush of the sanctuary and sneaking single-bite chocolate layer cakes and plastic cups of grape juice afterwards. When I became religious in my 20s, I credited my grandparents with lighting my Jewish spark, even though I went beyond their observances—not driving from sundown Friday until three stars twinkled in the Saturday night sky and eating only kosher food, in restaurants and strict homes. That ruled out my grandparents' home.

"Are you never going to eat in our house again?" Grandpa asked me one cold winter night. The son of Orthodox immigrants from Poland, Grandpa revered ritual but compromised to bring people together. A candle flickered on our restaurant table, casting shadows against the white breadbasket napkin. Menus lay at the table edge. I would have the steak.

"I'm religious because of you," I whispered.

"What a legacy we're leaving," he said, hugging Grandma.

But it wasn't so easy. Cooking, food, the quest for control over the family table, brought us together as well as it ripped us apart.

Identity comes from so many places—my parents gave me fashion- and business-sense and a knowledge of the world while my grandparents grounded me in ancient traditions. As Hanukkah approaches, and Jews everywhere recall the destruction of the holy Temple by the Greeks and the subsequent miracle of a day's worth of oil burning for eight, so they could adequately rebuild, I think of the destructions and rebuildings that take place in our lives every day.

I'm lucky because, after a decade of being religious, I found a way to be respectful of tradition AND balanced—eating once again at the family table, making compromises as my family did so that we could all be together. That gift of family, of knowing who I am in a context of people, is priceless.

But there have been other gifts, too, like the creased, weathered cookbooks that Grandma gave to me after my grandfather passed away. My kitchen is home to 99 cookbooks with splattered, stained pages creased from years of beloved use. The titles I consider to be art. We decorate our rooms with details of what matters and in my home's heart, the warped white laminate kitchen where I bake zucchini- carrot bread and roll matzoh balls between wet hands, the counter on which my children sprinkle cheese and chopped olives onto homemade pizza and punch bread dough that we'll all shape into loaves, color comes from cookbooks.

Grandpa died after I'd been completely religious for four years. In his last months, he and Grandma cried when they looked at one another, knowing an end was near. Their sad passion was as intense as their joy singing over the Sabbath table. A few months after we buried Grandpa in the tree-lined cemetery, my grandmother gave me her cookbooks.

"Who would I cook for now?" she said.

I fingered the pile of four well-loved books. The binding had fallen apart on *The Settlement Cook Book*. Scotch-tape held the 1945 *Jewish Cook Book* together, while a rubber band secured *A Treasure for My Daughter*. Hidden in *Guide for the Jewish Homemaker* and *Jewish Cooking for Pleasure*, I found note cards with Grandma's handwriting, shortcuts and commentary in the margins.

More than using them, I run my fingers over their cracked covers, trying to remember my childhood, my history in the pages. Did I scribble in thick black crayon across the pages? Or were those thick lines from my mother's childhood, Grandma in an apron and spray-frozen hair? I imagine Mom and her siblings in the yard or down the street or later, me and my sister pounding the piano keys as the old dog Clancy lay on the blue living room carpet.

As a child, my religion was food more than prayer and in a way it still is: velvety brisket strips in a bubbling tomato sauce and satiny chicken soup with fluffy matzoh balls; gefilte fish balls with hats of soft carrot, mashed fried cow's liver, and a shining, jewel-toned jell-o mold with fruit inside. The table—my grandmother's, my mother's, my aunts', mine—holds china and white linens, as the kitchen emanates the coming meal's sweet husky scent. On Passover, the crowning moment at the seder table for me is not songs or stories but Grandma's light-as-air strawberry fluff dolloped atop sponge-cake.

When I took on religion, I was really immersing myself in the world of my ancestors. Tradition is the ultimate gift, I now know, which is why I lay in bed at night, recounting the way my grandfather made salad so my children will know this important part of him. They'll never touch his hands or hear his belly laugh, but at least they'll know the tastes he loved.

A friend once told me that Jews should be observant, first and foremost, because God told us to follow the ancient ways. That's not why I do it. I believe there is wisdom in all ways of living Jewishly and for me, the hours I spend in my kitchen, whipping eggs, mixing vegetables, roasting chicken with half-a-lemon inside, zest pressed into its skin, are some of the most important ways that I live my heritage.

Some nights, I try Grandma's recipes. I've mashed canned salmon with onion, paprika, cornflake crumbs and a well-beaten egg for patties, a favorite *Settlement Cook Book* recipe, modified with Grandma's notes. But most nights, I make modern favorites: vegetable-rich recipes or new ways to fry an age-old cut of meat.

"When I am grown up, will you come to my house?" my four-year-old daughter Eliana asks.

I nod and reach for her still-pudgy soft hand. "Of course. As much as I can," I say, thinking of the muffins and kugels and roasts and soups I'll make for her freezer. Just the way, when I was a new college graduate working in Manhattan, Grandma sent a clothing box filled with her velvety sugar-dusted brownies. I ate half a dozen, then took them to my office. Colleagues gathered around my desk until the box was empty, sharing their stories about family and food.

In the kitchen, Eliana stands on a chair next to me, tearing lettuce leaves into a wooden bowl. I chop scallions and tomatoes; she tastes a cucumber slice before scattering the rest over the salad. When I put garlic, mustard, oil and spices in a jar for dressing, she shakes it hard, her long blond hair swishing back and forth. Even my baby, Shaya, stands on a chair beside me, dipping his finger in batter for a taste. Dinner is salad, quiche, soup from the freezer. My eldest, Asher, will eat slices of smoked cheese and turn up his nose at what I've made. Eliana will try a little bit of everything.

Regardless of our preferences and personal tastes, my children will know that one of the best ways we give to others is to create heart-warming meals that not only fill our bellies, they sustain our souls.

Mary Rose O'Reilley

KEY LIME PIE
(for Katie Guthrie)

Commas of lime in sugar and milk,
suspension, mild on the tongue
as memory of being filled,
or if you never were full before,
now is the moment—
be born again,
trailing, for all I care,
Augustine, Ambrose, all of those guys—

Aquinas, sit here, eat this pie.
Each one's longing to feel
a belly round with surfeit,
figuring out at last
one of the why's we came for:
key lime pie.

Tumble with me, Augustine,
out of the pear tree of self-hate.
Here is a Buddha-pie your African grin
can barely take in. Here is a radical
homecoming pie. Aquinas,
it runs down your chin.
You will never again
have to be clever or even good.

Taste the green skin of logos
wanting to kiss your tongue.
You are undone, like a child
gone feral to smell grass,
murmuring here it is,
all I have longed for
at last, at last.

Joan Chittister, OSB

TABLE FELLOWSHIP

When you're a novice you begin to notice the little things: how a novice mistress pulls at her veil when she's amused, for instance; or how she pulls on her scapular when she isn't; how the sister in the wardrobe stands with her arms spread on the countertop if she's not too busy to be bothered; how the portress's tone of voice changes when you ask her to page a person for the fourth time in a row. What our novices noticed was that there were always raisins in the oatmeal on "speaking days," feast days great enough, that is, to justify the community's talking at meals.

There were eleven "speaking days" on the community calendar in those days, not enough to bother memorizing the list, but enough to warrant keeping your eyes on the oatmeal. "What if," the novices assigned to kitchen duty wondered, "you put raisins in the oatmeal on *feria* or ordinary days? Would the prioress think it was a feast day and automatically say the prayer that signaled permission to speak at breakfast?"

So one day they tried it. Mother Sylvester looked at her oatmeal, looked up at her council sitting nearby, looked back down at the oatmeal, pushed a raisin or two to the side of the bowl to inspect them more closely, looked up at the community, frowned a little frown, stared at the raisins—and gave praise.

I remember the happy buzz of excitement in the dining room, the confusion at the head table as prioress and council checked their *ordos* and their pocket calendars, the giggle at the novices' table—and the look of horror on the novice mistress's face. I also remember that

140

it never happened again. But the point had been made: Feast days have something to do with food. The celebration of life has something to do with food. Food is the glue and the center of human community making.

I began to understand life and community and celebration and the Eucharist a great deal better.

Let us acknowledge the source of life,

source of nourishment.

May we protect the bountiful earth

that it may continue to sustain us,

And let us seek sustenance

for all who dwell in the world.

MARCIA FALK

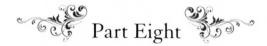

Part Eight

COMPOST

NO BEGINNING AND NO END

Food begins in the garden and ultimately ends up in the garden. It's one big cycle from seed to plant to food to compost to nourish a seed, and emblematic of our spiritual cycles—no beginning and no end. You've been given just enough. This is illustrated through three different faith perspectives—the Qur'an, the writings of Buddhist scholar Daisetz Teitaro Suzuki, and the Hindu Upanishads. In the Qur'an, "He does not love the wasters" resonates with the theme in Suzuki's selection wherein the Master of the Kuei-shan monastery admonishes the granary keeper to, "Be careful not to think slightingly of the one grain of rice, for hundreds of thousands of grains all come out of it." The passage from the Upanishads, "By food they grow, and to food they return," echoes the tones of all the pieces, which look at the practical, the everyday, but their messages expand to the cosmic.

Author and filmmaker Kristen Wolf applies this notion to our modern-day lives with "The Parable of the Squash." She learns through her own "loaves and fishes" epiphany "to seek out the intrinsic 'Enough-ness' in our lives, be it in food, water, clothing, possessions, or money."

The miracle of enough is just what Haven Kimmel reveals in her memoir excerpt, "Diner," where she realizes that, perhaps, as her mother tells her, she has all she needs already: "It was an Indian summer afternoon in Indiana, a rare gift. We walked home slowly. I thought Mom might be wrong about me having all I needed, but just at the moment, I had no need to complain."

Alisa Smith and J. B. MacKinnon, who spent a year eating only foods produced within one hundred miles of their home, contribute the final selection to this chapter. Their journey began with a transcendent dinner crafted from whatever was at hand, an aspiration, and a question: "Was there some way to carry this meal into the rest of our lives?"

Every action, every prayer, every thought returns to us, just as every discarded orange peel, uneaten fish stick, or piece of burnt toast ends up somewhere. Understanding the connection—this reality of no beginning and no end, no separation between the seed and the flower and the rotted fruit—is the essence of how the cycles of food can demonstrate what's holy. It's a way to realize that our place in the universe, although we consider ourselves to be at the top of the food chain, is circular rather than linear. This recognition puts us on par with the mustard seed and the grain of rice—we are all holy. Seeing our role in the cycle offers an opportunity to glimpse our unity with all things, big or small, cosmic or mundane.

HE DOES NOT LOVE THE WASTERS

He is the One who established gardens, trellised and untrellised, and palm trees, and crops with different tastes, and olives, and pomegranate—fruits that are similar, yet dissimilar. Eat from their fruits, and give the due alms on the day of harvest, and do not waste anything. He does not love the wasters.

Daisetz Teitaro Suzuki

A WORM IN THE RICE

One of the principles governing the life at Zendo ... is not to waste. This applies with special emphasis to cookery where the vegetables or grains of rice and barley are always liable to be thoughtlessly thrown away. Chu, of Shi Shuang, who acted as keeper of the granary at Kuei-shan, was one day found putting rice through a sieve, when the master of the Kuei-shan monastery appeared and said: "Don't scatter the grains for they come from our kind-hearted donors."

Chu: "No, master, I won't scatter them about."

The master looked around and picked up a grain of rice from the ground and said: "You say you don't scatter them about; if so, where does this grain come from?"

Chu remained silent; the master continued: "Be careful not to think slightingly of the one grain of rice, for hundreds of thousands of grains all come out of it."

Chu: "May I ask where this one grain comes from?"

The master made no special answer to this, but laughing heartily went back to his own quarters. In the evening he came out into the Hall and said: "O monks, there is a worm in our rice."

From the Taittiriya Upanishad Part III

FOOD IS GOD

Bhirigu went to his father, Varuna,
And asked respectfully: "What is Brahman?"

Varuna replied: "First learn about food,
Breath, eye, ear, speech, and mind; then seek to know
That from which these are born, by which they live,
For which they search, and to which they return.
That is Brahman."

Bhrigu meditated and found that food
Is Brahman. From food are born all creatures
By food they grow, and to food they return.

Kristen Wolf

THE PARABLE OF THE SQUASH

Last night that time rolled around again. As it always does. You know the time I'm talking about: Dinnertime.

And last night, having spent a day at home working, I discovered after checking the refrigerator that there was little to eat. On any other winter night, my partner and I might have bundled up for the drive into town and the familiar hunt for victuals. But there was snow on the road. And ice. So I decided to get creative.

I began by searching every drawer, cabinet, and shelf until my eyes fell upon a single butternut squash squatting in our fruit bowl. I stared at the unlikely suspect, a super-sized Weeble of the vegetable world. Curious, I picked it up and heaved it from hand to hand. It was small, but heavy. Maybe I could make something out of it?

My partner walked by, eyeing me suspiciously. In our home, there is precious little faith in my kitchen abilities, and my deep contemplation of a single squash at dinnertime wasn't winning me any points. But I felt hopeful.

Setting myself to the task at hand, I pulled a container of homemade vegetable stock from the freezer to thaw. I then peeled the entire squash, watching the waxy slivers of cream-colored rind fall away to reveal the bright buttery-orange interior. I thought about the metaphor of looking beneath the skin of something, and the startling surprises that often reward this effort. But there was no time to wax poetic.

Next, I poured a thin layer of olive oil in a pot, heated it, tossed in diced onions and sprinkled them with curry powder and a dash of cayenne as they cooked. When the onions had browned, I dropped in the block of vegetable stock, which melted quickly. To the liquid I added chunks of squash and allowed the whole thing to simmer. After a half-an-hour, and delivering a glass of wine and a few words of re-assurance to my partner, I strained the squash and onions from the broth, dropped the chunks in a food processor and stirred the day-glo paste back into the broth.

The result was a vat of rich soup, thick enough to stand a wooden spoon in. My partner toasted my culinary victory as we bent over our large bowls. Finding the meal more than edible, we each went back for seconds. After our feast, I returned to the kitchen. Dried rivulets and splatters of squash soup covered the outside of the pot, making it look every bit like a Jackson Pollack. Amazingly, the pot was still more than half full!

Over the next week, we would occasionally pull the pot from the refrigerator to heat up a ladleful for lunch, dinner, or a midday snack. And yet, no matter how much we ate, there always seemed to be enough soup left for another meal or two.

My partner and I eventually nicknamed it "the Loaves and Fishes" soup.

As the meals continued, I thought a lot about that butternut. And how richly, and unexpectedly, a single vegetable, and a little broth, could feed two adults. Before that night, I would never have believed that one squash could be enough. Then I realized something. I had no idea what enough, as in Enough, actually meant.

Enough, I speculated, was enough, right? Wasn't that the truism? Enough meant having whatever was required. No more and no less. It meant having a sufficient amount of whatever was necessary to be satiated in some way. It meant that when a need arose, one availed oneself of the amount necessary to sustain life, and then carried on. And this being the case, having Enough was a finite moment with a clear beginning and ending.

I remembered watching a lioness, panting under a tree in Africa, her chin stained with blood, having just fed herself, and her three cubs, on a young gazelle. And I remembered how the herds of surviving gazelles grazed close to this mother, knowing with confidence that she was satisfied, and would not be hunting for many hours. That day I learned the rule of the savannah, a law of instinct, a universal covenant that cannot be broken: No animal takes more than it needs. The lioness could have easily taken more prey. But she didn't. She had had Enough.

There is, it would seem, no corollary for this law of instinct in our current human experience. How, I wondered, can "enough be enough" when the world is littered with advertisements imploring us to consume more? How can enough be enough when, in a world where we have more than we need, the media assures us that we don't have enough, that we're not "keeping up"? I recently called a computer company to purchase a $20 software upgrade. Within seconds of assessing the configuration of my system, the young sales associate insisted that I get an entirely new computer with triple the processor speed and all the latest wingy-dos. I gagged. My computer suited me fine! It met my every need gallantly. It was Enough. But the man on the other end of the phone was working awfully hard to convince me that what I had was nowhere near sufficient. I needed more. More than Enough.

Our culture seems to have lost touch with the emotion of satisfaction. In our world, why should one butternut squash be Enough when we can go downtown and choose from a plethora of local eateries churning out hamburgers, enchiladas, steaks, spare ribs, swordfish, and chicken? In that same vein, why should I bother to repair and extend the life of my "old" car when the dealers' lots are flooded with shiny new models in the full rainbow of colors? Why should I have only one phone/TV/stereo in my home when there are enough available for me to have two, three, or four? And why should a cup of water be enough to brush my teeth when two gallons can spill, virtually unnoticed, from the faucet while I floss? (Even though those two gallons are more than most families on earth have for a week's worth of drinking, cleaning, and cooking.)

Why, indeed.

When I really woke up and thought about it, after that night of warm butternut soup, I felt a fear that shook me to the ground. I thought of my own buying and consuming habits. How easily I had been led to believe in a worldview that says, "Enough is never enough because there's plenty more where that came from!" There is no doubt that this criminal, and unsustainable, worldview is perpetuated, even promoted, by our corporate leaders in their reckless pursuit of profit. But it takes two to tango, and there are other guilty parties: you and I, entrenched in our habit of day-to-day gluttony, unconsciously consuming as though the Earth were here for no other reason than our personal plundering, and believing the producers who assure us that this is so.

Nowadays, for better or for worse, I am compelled to measure the appropriateness of my daily behavior by that one uneven vegetable—the butternut squash. I reuse and recycle everything from batteries to plastic cups. I turn off the water in between tasks. I create meals from scraps. But perhaps more important than the day-to-day alterations I have made to my behavior, is my adoption of the belief that the great and holy concept of Enough really does exist, and is more easily attainable than I ever suspected. Isn't that, after all, what the Parable of the Loaves and Fishes was all about?

In my reading, this story isn't simply about a messiah performing a miracle, or a celebration of faith, but it is a teaching from a wise soul reminding us to seek out the intrinsic "Enough-ness" in our lives, be it in food, water, clothing, possessions, or money.

I laughed to imagine the shock on peoples' faces when Jesus was able to feed thousands from five loaves of bread and two fish. It reminded me of the shock on my own face when a single miraculous squash provided several meals. And what was amply demonstrated, for both myself and for those listening to Jesus, was that Enough, and all of its soft contentment, could be drawn from less than we believed. Much less. And that the phenomenon we experienced, of drawing more from less, was not a miracle; it was a shift in perspective.

In my own life, I have found that to live by the rule of Enough, is to live in a world where contentment is not only possible but frequent. It is a place where the satisfied feeling of being "well-fed" lasts. And from this place, I can see the folly of striving for more than Enough. It is like trying to fill a bucket with a hole in it. It can never suffice. Never satisfy. It can only leave me in a state of constant hunger and craving. And in the panicked state of want, I will seek to take more even when doing so costs me my happiness and, worse, leads to the destruction of the elements that sustain me. It is a living death. A chronic dissatisfaction. A slow, greedy suicide.

The older I get, I'm finding, the more unlikely the sources of my lessons.

And now, it seems, even lopsided vegetables have become revered teachers. Of course there is no doubt in my mind that many will think me absurd, simple-minded, and out-dated. They will ask, why do I settle for the wisdom of a vegetable when I can choose from a limitless parade of enlightened gurus, creeds, philosophies, messiahs, and workshops, with all the attending accoutrements?

All I know is that I am grateful for what the butternut squash has shown me.

For the taste of that rare and lovely feeling of satisfaction it has offered. And for me, in this particular moment, the wisdom of one vegetable is Enough.

Haven Kimmel

DINER

There are a finite number of times one can safely climb the same tree in a single day; after that point the whole venture becomes meaningless, and potentially dangerous. I had climbed my favorite tree, an oak that had a perfect bottom-shaped well where the big limbs began, about five times. I was getting casual with gravity, and had begun dismounting higher and higher, when I realized that I was aware of my stomach.

I was hungry. I walked into the house, which was so surprisingly empty. My sister had married only a few months before and was now living down the street; my brother was not a person I would consider in such a situation; my father had gone to one of the many mysterious places he had to be; and my mother, who we all trusted for so many years to remain faithfully in her place on the couch, was working.

She had taken a job waitressing at the little restaurant on Broad Street that sat diagonally from the drugstore. From the outside it just looked like a shotgun house. There were even checkered curtains in the window and a front stoop for sitting. Mom had only been working there a few days, and only the lunch shift, but her absence was alarming.

Our kitchen was really a part of our den—separated only by a "breakfast bar" at which no breakfast was ever taken—and I stood in the strange nether world between the den and the kitchen, staring. I never entered the kitchen if I could avoid it, and even as I stood there, deeply worried, I could hear mice skittering around in the oven.

155

I ran back outside and stood on the front porch, bark dangling from my sweatshirt and my hair. Oh, I was so hungry. I was hungry, hungry, and at what appeared to be a desperate time: the Newmans were not at the gas station, Rose and her family were out of town, and my sister had gone to New Castle. I had no money. I couldn't think of how to steal any. My mom was completely gone.

I sat on the porch steps and contemplated, my stomach growling and grumbling. If I went back in the house I would have to face the kitchen, and if I stayed outside I would surely expire.

I went inside, and slowly, fearfully, walked across the sticky kitchen floor to the refrigerator. The inside of the refrigerator was no better than any other part of the kitchen, but I was able to locate a bag of carrots, which I grabbed, slamming the door behind me. I took them outside and whittled off the grubby outsides with my pocket knife and set to eating them. They were pretty good, for vegetables. I ate one, and then another, and probably a third and fourth, distractedly, until I noticed the whole bag was empty and I wasn't hungry anymore. In fact, my stomach felt like a little carrot rock.

I tried lying down in the yard and moaning out loud, which seemed to comfort the people who died on soap operas. The leaves and twigs snapped and poked in an unfriendly way. When I stood up to head for the house, I found that I felt even worse. I realized I needed my mother.

The walk to the diner was a long and treacherous one. I periodically had to stop and sit down in the grass to gather enough strength to go on. The sun pounded down on me, so that by the time I reached the front door I was stooped over like the emphysemic old man my grandma was married to, Pappy Catt, and I was clutching my stomach. It took all of my willpower to straighten up enough to open the restaurant's front door.

Mom was walking out of the back where the desserts were kept, carrying a piece of pie to a man who was sitting at the counter drinking coffee and looking at a map. One look at him told me he was from nowhere near Mooreland. He was wearing a suit, which was, as far as I knew, a habit practiced only by men who sold insurance, like Rose's dad. Mom gestured for me to sit down at the counter, and then she ducked into the kitchen.

Obviously she had not noticed how terribly aggrieved I was. I stooped over to the counter and slid onto the stool right next to the businessman, even though the rest of the diner was empty. He looked at me without speaking or smiling, then turned back to his map.

My stomach just flat-out somersaulted. I called out, "Mom!"

"I'll be right there!" she yelled back.

I put my head down on my arms and took some deep breaths. When I was able to I shouted again, "Mom! I need some water!"

The man at the counter, perturbed, pushed his water my direction. I sat up straight enough to take a drink, raised the glass to my lips, and vomited, right into the water. What the glass couldn't hold had just fallen neatly on to the counter, and it was nothing but shredded carrots. After I finished making that one last little heave that concludes a throwing up, I found myself quite interested in the contents of the glass, and turned it toward the window to hold it up to the light.

The man next to me dropped his fork in an unnecessarily dramatic way, then grabbed his map and headed for the door, dropping money on the floor on the way out.

My mom came around the corner and saw me looking down into the carrot water. "Oh, sweetheart! What happened?!"

"There was nothing to eat at our house but carrots!" I said, indignant. "So I ate them and got sick and came down here to try and just get a glass of water, and the man sitting there gave me his and I threw up in it. That's the throw-up right there."

"I see it. Are you feeling better?"

"I feel fine. What kind of pie did I see you carrying earlier?"

Mom felt my head and cleaned up the mess. We both declared that it was one of the more interesting sights we'd ever beheld, and I told her a few more times about how the carrots had just come straight up and so neatly into the glass, like I had planned it. She brought me a piece of warm sugar-cream pie, and it occurred to me that for warm sugar-cream pie I'd throw up every day.

When I stepped out of the restaurant to go home, I noticed that Sammy Bellings was sitting on her front steps next door. I ambled over and sat down next to her. Sammy had blond hair and very slanty cat eyes, and her skin was a brown color. She was one of seventeen kids living in the little house between the diner and an abandoned grocery store; some of the kids belonged only to the father, and some only to the mother, and some had gotten made together, but nobody really knew who was whose. Sammy didn't often wear panties, so I was quite familiar with her brown bottom. It was something of a scandal at school.

"Hey," she said, waving.

"Hey. I just threw up a bunch of carrots in a glass of water," I told her, pointing toward the restaurant.

"Why did you eat a bunch of carrots?" she asked, wrinkling up her nose.

"Was the only thing I could find. I was starving to death."

"Yeah," she said, nodding sympathetically. "That happened to me once. I was walking around the house saying I'm so hungry I'm so hungry and my ma kept saying I had to wait until dinner. We weren't gonna eat for hours. So I was saying I'm so hungry I'm so hungry and then I found this bag of potato chips and I took them out in the backyard and ate the whole bag and then I puked it all back up and the dog came over and ate it."

Now I didn't know what Sammy meant when she said she went out in the backyard, because what they had was a square of dirt that butted up to the alley, but I didn't say anything. The detail about the dog made the whole story convincing.

"I think moms ought to just feed you when you're hungry," I said, as if I were making a declaration.

Sammy snorted. "Tell that to my mom."

My own mother came out of the diner, finished with her shift. I saw her and scampered down off Sammy's stoop.

"See ya later!" I said, waving behind me, and she waved back.

I caught up with my mom, who was still wearing her apron with the big pocket in the front. I snuck my hand into it.

"Got any money in there?" I asked, waggling my eyebrows at her.

"You don't need any money," she said, swatting my hands away and pulling me close to her at the same time. "You've got all you need already."

It was an Indian summer afternoon in Indiana, a rare gift. We walked home slowly. I thought Mom might be wrong about me having all I needed, but just at the moment, I had no need to complain.

Alisa Smith and J. B. MacKinnon

ONE BEAUTIFUL MEAL

The year of eating locally began with one beautiful meal and one ugly statistic.

First, the meal. What we had on hand, really, was a head of cabbage. Deep inside its brainwork of folds it was probably nourishing enough, but the outer layers were greasy with rot, as though the vegetable were trying to be a metaphor for something. We had company to feed, and a three-week-old cabbage to offer them.

It wasn't as though we could step out to the local megamart. We—Alisa and I—were at our "cottage" in northern British Columbia, more honestly a drafty, jauntily leaning, eighty-year-old homestead that squats in a clearing between Sitka spruce and western redcedar [*sic*] trees large enough to crush it into splinters with the sweep of a limb. The front door looks out on a jumble of mountains named after long-forgotten British lords, from the peaks of which you can see, just to the northwest, the southern tip of the Alaska Panhandle. There is no corner store here. In fact, there is no electricity, no flush toilet, and no running water but for the Skeena River rapids known as the Devil's Elbow. They're just outside the back door. Our nearest neighbor is a black bear. There are also no roads. In fact, the only ways in or out are by canoe, by foot over the distance of a half-marathon to the nearest highway, or by the passenger train that passes once or twice a day, and not at all on Tuesdays. So: we had a cabbage, and a half-dozen mouths to feed for one more autumn evening. Necessity, as they say, can be a mother.

I can't remember now who said what, or how we made the plan, or even if we planned at all. What I know is that my brother David, a strict vegetarian, hiked to the mouth of Fiddler Creek, which straight-lines out of a bowl of mountains so ancient they make you feel perpetually re-born, and reeled in an enormous Dolly Varden char. Our friends Kir and Chandra, who are the sort of people who can tell a Bewick's wren from a rufous-crowned sparrow by ear, led a party into the forest and returned with pound upon pound of chanterelle, pine, and hedgehog mushrooms. I rooted through the tall grass to find the neglected garden plot where months earlier, we had planted garlic and three kinds of po-tato; each turned up under the spade, as cool and autonomous as teenagers. Alisa cut baby dandelion leaves, while her mother picked ap-ples and sour cherries from an abandoned orchard, and rose hips from bushes that were attempting to swallow the outhouse. The fruit we steeped in red wine—all right, the wine came from Australia. Everything else we fried on the woodstove, all in a single huge pan.

It was delicious. It was a dinner that transcended the delicate fresh-ness of the fish, the earthy goodness of the spuds that had sopped up the juices of mushrooms and garlic. The rich flavors were the evening's shallowest pleasure. We knew now, that out there in the falling dark-ness of the river and the forest spoke a subtle language we had only begun to learn. It was the kind of meal that, when the plates were clean, led some to dark corners to sleep with the hushing of the wind, and oth-ers to drink mulled wine until our voices had climbed an octave and fi-nally deepened, in the small hours, into whispers. One of the night's final questions, passed around upon faces made golden by candlelight: Was there some way to carry this meal into the rest of our lives?

Earth Water Air and Fire combined to make this food.

Numberless beings gave their lives and labor that we may eat.

May we be nourished that we may nourish life.

JOAN HALIFAX ROSHI

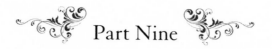

Part Nine

GRACE

COMMUNION

At my family's church—Saint Marks Church-in-the-Bowery, in New York City—Communion is performed by standing in a circle that expands to include the entire congregation. Each person receives the bread, and then the wine, from his or her neighbor on one side and serves it to his or her neighbor on the other, passing it all the way around the circle. The circle expands to include everyone at the service. No matter how many times I engage in this ritual, I can't stop being overwhelmed by the power and beauty of it—the metaphor that people can create a table big enough to include everyone and being certain that everyone at that table has enough to eat.

The food we eat and how we eat it impacts the whole world. It is in the act of sharing it, however, that both author Laurie Colwin and Sri Guru Granth Sahib Ji realize divinity. Colwin discovers, at the Olivieri Center for Homeless Women, that everyone, no matter their circumstances, has something to give. Colwin writes, "There were [homeless] ladies who helped peel potatoes and one who washed the pots every day. When I asked her why she did this unrewarding job, she said: 'I feel God has been very good to me and I like to pay back.'" Colwin shows us that by feeding those who have less than we do, we're feeding our own souls and initiating a cycle of generosity through which others may benefit by receiving or giving as well.

Poet Lawrence Raab expresses the joyful in creating one dinner that expands to become enough food for everyone, everywhere: "You have only to say their names, / ask them inside. Everyone will find a place / at your table." German novelist Elias Canetti sees unity among those who share food from a common dish, explaining, "The bond between the eaters is strongest when it is *one* animal they partake of, one body which they knew as a living unit, or one loaf of bread."

As writer Lynn L. Caruso nurses her child, she reflects on the wonders of the cycles all around her, and how she plays a part in the perpetuation of those cycles. Caruso voices how giving birth, flowers from seed, milk from the body, and a grandmother's love are all part of the greater picture, capturing the cycle of birth, love, and rebirth—seed to garden to food to seed again.

Sara Miles, author and founder of a food pantry in San Francisco, describes glory in terms of Christian Communion and expresses wonder and clarity at her epiphany that Communion is far more than mere ritual. It includes recognizing hunger and feeding people. The stories of Jesus demonstrate to her that, "All of it pointed to a force stronger than the anxious formulas of religion: a radically inclusive love that accompanied people in the most ordinary of actions—eating, drinking, walking—and stayed with them, through fear, even past death. That love meant giving yourself away, embracing outsiders as family, emptying yourself to feed and live for others."

Writer and political activist Grace Paley gets to the heart of the matter in her introduction to the *Greenwich Village Peace Center Cookbook*, as she reminds us that there are many ways to share a meal, "since it's impossible to invite *everyone* to supper."

Coming full circle, from seed to slaughterhouse to eating to serving to celebrating to sharing, we end up in the garden, or more precisely the rice paddy, with poet Mary Oliver's "Rice," in which she urges us against complacency:

> I don't want you just to sit down at the table.
> I don't want you just to eat, and be content.
> I want you to walk out into the fields
> where the water is shining, and the rice has risen.
> I want you to stand there, far from the white tablecloth.
> I want you to fill your hands with the mud, like a blessing.

And so we return, from the tangible bread, to the manifestation as the body, to the aspiration of spirit. Communion in terms of striving to make sure that everyone, everywhere, is nourished physically and spiritually starts with grace and returns to grace; the end is the beginning.

Sri Guru Granth Sahib Ji—Ang 1245

THE PATH

He alone treads the path of righteousness ... who earns his bread with honest labor and shares it with others.

Laurie Colwin

FEEDING THE MULTITUDES

[Fourteen years later,] I found myself in the kitchen of the Olivieri Center for Homeless Women, on Manhattan's West Side in the heart of the fur district. The Olivieri Center is technically a drop-in center, but women are allowed to sleep there, on the floor. It is two blocks from Pennsylvania Station, seven blocks south of the Port Authority Bus Terminal and across town from Grand Central Station. In all of these places, destitute women live—in the ladies' room, in secret places under the tracks, in the waiting rooms. Many of them find their way to Olivieri, where they can shower, get fresh clothes and eat three meals a day. If they stick around, they can talk to a caseworker who will try to straighten out their entitlements—many women receive supplemental security income, a form of social security for the disabled—or help to get them on public assistance. They can be seen by a doctor and sent to a free clinic.

When I started to volunteer one hot June morning, the cook, an unflappable, handsome woman named Jean Delmoor, was serving lunch to 120 ladies.

Until you get the notion to volunteer, you do not know who your population is. Some people read to the blind or take deaf children to baseball games. Some people make home visits to the elderly or work with children or runaways. I did not know until I started that my population would be chronically homeless, mentally ill women.

For a couple of months I stayed behind the counter with Jean and performed the services of her sous-chef. I mixed and chopped and fetched and scraped carrots and peeled potatoes. Little by little I got the hang of the place. I got to know the ladies and the ladies began to know me.

None of these women was in very good shape. In addition to schizophrenia, paranoia, psychosis and delusions, these women suffered from diabetes, congestive heart failure and leg ulcerations, the scourge of people who never lie down to sleep. They had neglected teeth, respiratory problems, lice, scabies and TB. There were pregnant women who refused or never received prenatal care. One woman, in fact, delivered on the floor without saying a word. When the caseworker on night duty went to attend to her before the ambulance came, the only words she spoke were: "Do you have a cigarette?"

Some of these women had been homeless for years. Many were former mental patients although there were battered wives, women terrorized out of the Single Room Occupancy hotel rooms by landlords hot to gentrify, mothers burned out of their apartments, or thrown out by boyfriends, husbands and family.

Not one of them was like another. They were and are the most surprising group of people I have ever encountered, and not a single assumption can be made about them except that they are all living in a horrible way. They were old, young and middle-aged. Some women had advanced degrees. Some had hardly finished the fifth grade. They were black, white, Hispanic, of every religion and creed. They came from everywhere on the face of the earth, and one of them was a person who was waiting for a transsexual operation and was therefore not allowed in either the men's or the women's shelter. She or he, wearing mules with pom-poms, lived for a while at the Olivieri Center.

But all of them had to be fed and I was happy to be the person ladling lunch onto plates or drawing coffee into Styrofoam cups from a huge urn.

One morning in the fall I turned up and found the kitchen empty.

"Where's Jean?" I asked Juan, who was half security guard and half maintenance man.

"It's her day off," he said.

"Who's cooking?" I asked brightly.

"I guess you," said Juan.

A chill went over my heart.

"How many ladies am I cooking for?"

Juan consulted a sheet.

"About ninety-eight," he said.

I sat down on a milk crate. Suddenly I, who fussed if more than six people came to a dinner party, was responsible for feeding lunch to ninety-eight women.

Downstairs in the pantry were enormous cans of stewed tomatoes, and similarly enormous cans of tomato paste. With Juan to help I brought up onions and spaghetti plus government-surplus Cheddar cheese. In two hours I had made two huge stockpots of tomato sauce and boiled thirty pounds of pasta.

I made my mother's old-fashioned baked spaghetti. The idea is to have much more sauce than pasta and to embed the spaghetti in the sauce. You then bake it in the oven under a thick crust of cheese. I filled four steam-table trays and was vastly relieved to see that it was a hit.

From then on, Jean took her day off on my day on, and I had the kitchen to myself, more or less. I found cooking on the Olivieri's six-burner Garland restaurant stove a pleasure, and I spent many waking hours wondering what to make for large numbers of people.

I made chili, baked beans, macaroni and cheese, baked ziti, borscht, cabbage salad, pasta salad, vegetable stew and toasted cheese. One of the ladies' favorite lunches was baked potato, cheese, salad and fruit, a nice lunch for a winter day.

I then got the brilliant idea to make an Irish dish called colcannon, a mixture of spring onions, cabbage and mashed potatoes. The result was not a success, and one of my favorite ladies, who wore fuzzy sweaters, beads, and had a voice like Lauren Bacall's, came up to me and said: "Lunch today, honey. A *disaster*!"

There were ladies who were vegetarian and others furious at not getting meat for lunch. Some women came up and chatted and some never made eye contact. There were ladies who helped peel potatoes and one who washed the pots every day. When I asked her why she did this unrewarding job, she said: "I feel God has been very good to me and I like to pay back."

Lawrence Raab

SINCE YOU ASKED

Since you asked, let's make it dinner
at your house—a celebration
for no reason, which is always
the best occasion. Are you worried
there won't be enough space, enough food?

But in a poem we can do anything we want.
Look how easy it is to add on rooms, to multiply
the wine and chickens. And while we're at it
let's take those trees that died last winter
and bring them back to life.

Things should look pulled together,
and we could use the shade—so even now
they shudder and unfold their bright new leaves.
And now the guests are arriving—everyone
you expected, then others as well:

friends who never became your friends,
the women you didn't marry, all their children.
And the dead—I didn't tell you
but they're always included in these gatherings—
hesitant and shy, they hang back at first

among the blossoming trees.
You have only to say their names,
ask them inside. Everyone will find a place
at your table. What more can I do?
The glasses are filled, the children are quiet.

My friend, it must be time for you to speak.

Elias Canetti

POTLATCH

A certain esteem for each other is clearly evident in all who eat together. This is already expressed by the fact of their *sharing*. The food in the common dish before them belongs to all of them together. Everyone takes some of it and sees that others take some too. Everyone tries to be fair and not to take advantage of anyone else. The bond between the eaters is strongest when it is *one* animal they partake of, one body which they knew as a living unit, or one loaf of bread.

Lynn L. Caruso

COMMUNION
(for Grandmother Margaret)

Stepping stone on stone
through her garden's gate, Margaret
finds us with her promises to spray
for worms in the fall, her fingers
thimbling deep into the wine of cherries
in the bowl she's brought to share, her silver
hair stitched with coral shells from the chestnut
tree, while my son nurses curled at my
breast, in one mystic inhale of *take,*
eat and do this in remembrance
of the afternoon beneath the lyric
blossoms of the chestnut tree where bees
drink their own sweet nectar from the stamen's
cup, and my son, this child who's seen
the underside of me, like a moonflower
knowing all there is to know of night,
fingers out with hands like startled stars,
to touch the ruby stain in his great
grandmother's palm, still clinging
to the cream of my body with his soft
mouth, and in this giving
and receiving, there is water
into wine.

Sara Miles

CROSSING II

Bit by bit, I was getting a picture, one that might very well have been incomprehensible to fellow Christians in stern fundamentalist Nigeria, or pro-life Colorado, or even other Episcopal parishes in San Francisco. Of course, just like them, I was becoming more and more convinced that I was right, and that what I had figured out about faith, on my own lovely little spiritual adventure, was going to uplift and sanctify and generally improve my life.

When I talked with my secular friends, I could make a thoughtful case for church as a site for social change, or earnestly analyze the denominational politics of Christianity, as if that was what I cared about. I tried to justify my interest in St. Gregory's by telling my wife Martha that understanding contemporary politics required understanding religion. I acted as if I were an interested reporter, and not really that hungry.

The reality was different: deep, nonrational, desiring.

Poking around in the Bible, I found clues about my deepest questions. Salt, grain, wine, and water; fig trees, fishermen, and farmers. There were Psalms about hunger and thirst, about harvests and feasting. There were stories about manna in the wilderness, and prophets fed by birds. There was God appearing in radiance to Ezekiel and handing him a scroll: "Mortal," he said, "eat this scroll," and Ezekiel swallowed the words, "sweet as honey," and knew God.

And then in the New Testament appeared the central, astonishing fact of Jesus, proclaiming that he himself was the bread of heaven. "Eat my flesh and drink my blood," he said. I thought how outrageous

Jesus was to the church of his time: he didn't wash before meals, he said the prayers incorrectly, he hung out with women, foreigners, the despised and unclean. Over and over, he told people not to be afraid. I liked all that, but mostly I liked that he said he was bread and told his friends to eat him.

As I interpreted it, Jesus invited notorious wrongdoers to his table, airily discarded all the religious rules of the day, and fed whoever showed up, by the thousands. In the end he was murdered for eating with the wrong people.

And then—here's where the story got irrational. I didn't exactly "believe" it, the way I believed in the boiling point of water, or photosynthesis, but it seemed true to me—wholly true, in ways that mere facts could never be. I believed this God rose from the dead to have breakfast with his friends.

I read about the crazy days after Jesus' arrest, death, and burial, when the terrified disciples were scattering, just as I'd seen peasants and revolutionaries run from the violence of soldiers in Latin America. A stranger hailed them on the road to Emmaus. They told him what had happened, and he explained it all by citing Scripture, recounting old prophecies in impressive detail. Then, according to the book, they came to a village and invited the stranger to eat with them, as the night was drawing near. He sat down at the table, took bread, and broke it. Suddenly "their eyes were opened," reported the book. "He made himself known in the breaking of bread, and they felt their hearts on fire." Then he vanished. In another story, he reappeared cooking food on the beach. In another, he showed up to tell his followers that he was hungry and wanted something to eat. They gave him a piece of fish.

All of it pointed to a force stronger than the anxious formulas of religion: a radically inclusive love that accompanied people in the most ordinary of actions—eating, drinking, walking—and stayed with them, through fear, even past death. That love meant giving yourself away, embracing outsiders as family, emptying yourself to feed and live for others. The stories illuminated the holiness located in mortal human bodies, and the promise that people could see God by cherishing all those different bodies the way God did. They spoke of a communion so much vaster than any church could contain: one I had sensed all my life could be expressed in the sharing of food, particularly with strangers.

I couldn't stop thinking about another story: Jesus instructing his beloved, fallible disciple Peter exactly how to love him: "Feed my sheep."

Jesus asked, "Do you love me?" Peter fussed: "Of course I love you."

"Feed my sheep."

Peter fussed some more.

"Do you love me?" asked Jesus again. "Then feed my sheep."

It seemed pretty clear. If I wanted to see God, I could feed people.

Grace Paley

PEACEMEAL

Because I believe in the oral tradition in literature, I have been opposed to cookbooks. But I must concede I missed my chance. My mother and grandmother died silent and intestate—as far as borscht and apple pie are concerned. Or is it possible that I wasn't listening, that I was down the block drinking chocolate sodas and watching gang fights, which, in my part of the Bronx, raged between the kids of the Third and Fourth International?

After that, there was the war, then at last the daily life of grownups for which supper is prepared every night. I entered that world without a cookbook, but with an onion, a can of tomato sauce, and a fistful of ground chuck. If I have progressed beyond that worried moment, it is not due to cookbooks but to nosiness and political friendships.

I know lots of these recipes, because in the forty-five minutes between work and a Peace Center meeting I have often had to call Mary or Karl and ask, "How the hell did you say I should do that fish?" I have also gathered some hot tips at the Resistance dinners, which we served once a week at the Peace Center to about a hundred young men who were *not* going to be part of the U.S. plan to torment and murder the Vietnamese people.

Certainly this cookbook is for people who are not so neurotically antiauthoritarian as I am—to whom one can say, "Add the juice of one lemon," without the furious response: "Is that a direct order?" This leads to the people who made this book. We are a local Peace Center in a public neighborhood. We have lived and worked in basements and lofts, churches and storefronts, and are now at St. Luke's Church.

Although I have not been very useful to the writing and editing of this cookbook, I now see it as a sensible action—since it's impossible to invite *everyone* to supper.

Mary Oliver

RICE

It grew in the black mud.
It grew under the tiger's orange paws.
Its stems thinner than candles, and as straight.
Its leaves like the feathers of egrets, but green.
The grains cresting, wanting to burst.
Oh, blood of the tiger.

I don't want you just to sit down at the table.
I don't want you just to eat, and be content.
I want you to walk out into the fields
where the water is shining, and the rice has risen.
I want you to stand there, far from the white tablecloth.
I want you to fill your hands with the mud, like a
    blessing.

WAYS TO SHARE YOUR MEAL

There are literally hundreds of organizations that enable us to share the bounty from our tables. Below is a sampling of various large-scale services, but the options are not limited to this list—its just a jumping-off point to give you some idea of the groups that need support from individuals who recognize hunger as a global issue.

America's Second Harvest
35 East Wacker, Suite 2000
Chicago, Illinois 60601
(800) 771-2303
www.secondharvest.org

Feed the Children
PO Box 36
Oklahoma City, Oklahoma 73101
(800) 627-4550
www.FeedtheChildren.org

God's Love We Deliver
166 Avenue of the Americas
New York, New York 10013
(212) 294-8100
www.godslovewedeliver.org

Heifer Project International
1 World Avenue
Little Rock, Arkansas 72202
(800) 422-0474
www.heifer.org

Mercy Corps
Dept. W, 3015 SW First Avenue
Portland, Oregon 97201
(888) 256-1900
www.mercycorps.org

Oxfam International
226 Causeway Street, 5th Floor
Boston, Massachusetts 02114
(800) 77-OXFAM
www.oxfam.org

Save Darfur Coalition
3246 Solutions Center
Lockbox #773246
Chicago, Illinois 60677
(800) 917-2034
www.savedarfur.org

The ONE Campaign
1400 Eye Street, NW, Suite 601
Washington, DC 20005
(202) 552-4990
www.one.org

✦ ACKNOWLEDGMENTS ✦

Holy guacamole! With great restraint, I've saved all of my puns for the end, so here's some food for thought:

Let's start with a fancy champagne toast to Wendy Schmalz. Best. Agent. Ever. And an excellent vintage of friend as well.

Mulled wine and crisp Vermont apples to the wonderful people at SkyLight Paths, especially Emily Wichland, Jessica Swift, and Jenny Buono, who added much to the flavor of this book.

An extra helping of gratitude to Adrian Butash and M. J. Ryan, whose *Bless This Food* and *A Grateful Heart* provided plates full of inspiration.

And thanks as well to Marc Poirier, Judy Singer Stevens, Fiona Thomas, Rev. John Denaro, and Bonnie Myotai Treace, Sensei, whose insights season these pages.

My cousin Julia got the banquet started by helping me gather the ingredients for the introduction and stuck around to help wash the dishes.

Pour my mom, Elsie, a decaf cappuccino with extra foam and that icky stuff in blue packets for first teaching me to really read poetry and for all the meals she prepared with presence and love, even if she once forgot to bake a piecrust. And my father, Bill, should join her by enjoying a perfectly executed Turkish coffee and thanks (again) for giving me that copy of *The Perennial Philosophy*.

Every meal should begin with grace and include art, and so, how fortunate I am to have two friends like Grace Lile and Arthur

Goldwag, whose generosity and genius infuse the pages of this book. I wouldn't be anywhere near to where I am without them.

No feast of gratitude would be complete without remembering all the dinner and writing tables where I've been invited to delight— you know who you are—thanks for saving me a place.

CREDITS

"Dharma Talk" by Geoffrey Shugen Arnold, Sensei. Blue Cliff Record, Case 74. Jinniu's Rice Pail. Featured in Mountain Record 22.1, Fall 2003.

A Native American Blessing from the Lama Foundation, San Cristobal, New Mexico.

Excerpt from *The Language of Baklava: A Memoir* © 2005 by Diana Abu-Jaber. Used by permission of Pantheon, a division of Random House, Inc.

Excerpt from *A Natural History of the Senses*, © 1990 by Diane Ackerman, published by Random House/Vintage, 1990.

"Deer Season" by Barbara Tayler Angell from *The Long Turn Toward the Light: Collected Poems* © Cleveland State University Poetry Center.

Michael Benedikt, "Beef Epitaph" from Night Cries © 1976 by Michael Benedikt, and reprinted with permission of Wesleyan University Press.

The Rev. Jennifer Baskerville-Burrows, "Lemon Love," used by permission of the author.

From *The Tassajara Bread Book*, by Edward Espe Brown, ©1970 by the Chief Priest, Zen Center, San Francisco, Revisions © 1986, 1995 by Edward Espe Brown. Reprinted by arrangement with Shambhala Publications, Inc.

Martin Buber from "Hassidim" © 1948 The Philosophical Library, 15 E 40th Street, 10016.

Buddhist Meal Gatha, "First, seventy-two labors ..." Village Zendo Version.

Excerpt from *Crowds and Power* by Elias Canetti, translated by Carol Stewart. Translation copyright © 1962, 1973 by Victor Gollancz, Ltd. Reprinted by permission of Farrar, Straus and Giroux, LLC.

Excerpt from *Listen with the Heart* by Joan Chittister © Sheed & Ward, an imprint of Rowman & Littlefield Publishers, Inc. in Lanham, MD. Reprinted by arrangement with Rowman & Littlefield Publishers, Inc.

Laurie Colwin, "Feeding the Multitudes" (from *Home Cooking*). Some portions originally published in magazines: *Gourmet, Inside, 7 Days*. Hardcover: Knopf, 1988. Paperback: HarperPerennial, 1993, 2000.

Amanda Cook, "Sugar-Frosted Memories." Copyright © 2008 by Amanda Cook. Reprinted with the permission of the author.

Mary Beth Crain with permission of the author.

Meister Eckhart from *Selected Writings* translated by Oliver Davies, copyright © Oliver Davies 1994, Penguin Books.

Kahlil Gibran From *The Prophet*.

From *Instructions to the Cook* by Bernard Glassman and Rick Fields, copyright © 1996 by Zen Community of New York and Rick Fields. Used by permission of Bell Tower, a division of Random House, Inc.

ABOUT THE CONTRIBUTORS

Diana Abu-Jaber is the author of two novels, *Crescent*, which was awarded the 2004 PEN Center USA Award for Literary Fiction, and *Arabian Jazz*, which won the 1994 Oregon Book Award. She is also the author of *The Language of Baklava: A Memoir*.

Diane Ackerman has written five collections of poems and several books of non-fiction, including *A Natural History of the Senses*.

Rabi'a al-Adwayiyya (c. 800) is considered a major saint of Islam and one of the central figures of the Sufi tradition.

Barbara Tanner Angell was the author of several collections of poetry, including *The Long Turn toward Light* and *Games and Puzzles*.

Geoffrey Shugen Arnold, Sensei, is the vice-abbot of Zen Mountain Monastery and the branch president of the Zen Center of New York City, and also manages the National Buddhist Prison Sangha. His teachings have appeared in various journals and in *The Best Buddhist Writing 2005*.

The Rev. Jennifer Baskerville-Burrows is an Episcopal priest and sustainable food advocate in Syracuse, New York. Her essay, "Lemon Love," is dedicated to Dana Peak, who understands well the endurance of love and friendship.

Michael Benedikt's (1935–2007) books of poetry include *Night Cries, Mole Notes, Sky*, and *The Body*. He was the recipient of a New York State Council for the Arts Grant, a Guggenheim Foundation Fellowship, and an NEA Fellowship.

Wendell Berry has been honored with the T. S. Elliot Award, the Aiken Taylor Award for poetry, and the John Hay Award of the Orion Society. Author of more than forty books of poetry, fiction, and essays, Berry has farmed a hillside in his native Henry County, Kentucky, with his wife, for more than forty years.

Edward Espe Brown began cooking and practicing Zen in 1965 and was or-dained as a priest by Shunryu Suzuki Roshi in 1971. He is the author of several cookbooks, including *The Tassajara Bread Book* and *Tomato Blessings and Radish Teachings*. He is also the editor of *Not Always So*, a collection of lectures by Shunryu Suzuki.

Martin Buber (1878–1965), a Jewish theologian and philosopher born in Vienna, is best known for his religious philosophy, expounded most famously in *I and Thou* and *Hassidism*.

Elias Canetti (1905–94) was awarded the Nobel Prize in literature in 1981. His most important works, all written in German, are the novel *Auto-Da-Fé* and *Crowds and Power*.

Lynn L. Caruso is a writer living in Spokane, Washington. Her work has been published in *Mothering* magazine and many other national journals and magazines. She is editor of *Blessing the Animals: Prayers and Ceremonies to Celebrate God's Creatures, Wild and Tame* and *Honoring Motherhood: Prayers, Ceremonies & Blessings* (both SkyLight Paths).

Joan Chittister, OSB, is the executive director of Benetvision, a research and resource center for contemporary spirituality, located in Erie, Pennsylvania. She is the author of more than twenty books, including *The Rule of Benedict* and *The Story of Ruth*.

Laurie Colwin (1944–1992) was the author of *Passion and Affect; Shine On, Bright and Dangerous Object; Happy All the Time; The Lone Pilgrim; Family Happiness; Another Marvelous Thing; Home Cooking; Goodbye without Leaving; More Home Cooking;* and *A Big Storm Knocked It Over*.

Amanda Cook began writing because words have always been a path of discovery for her. After a few pit stops in Africa and Australia, Amanda is back at home in Toronto with her large, noisy, extended family, which provides her with all the fodder she needs to discover the icing in the middle of everyday life.

Mary Beth Crain is the senior editor of *SoMA: A Review of Religion and Culture*. She is an established Southern California writer/editor and author of *A Widow, a Chihuahua, and Harry Truman;* and, with Terry Lynn Taylor, the best-selling *Angel Wisdom*. She is currently a contributing writer for *L.A. Weekly*.

Lama Surya Das is the founder of Western Buddhist Teachers Network and the author of several books, including *Awakening the Buddha Within; Awakening to the Sacred,* and *Awakening the Buddhist Heart*.

Ram Dass has served on the faculty at Stanford and Harvard universities. In the 1960s, he traveled to India, where he met his guru. Since then, he has pursued a variety of spiritual practices and written many books, including the international bestsellers *Be Here Now, Paths to God*, and *How Can I Help?*

Marc David is a nutritional psychologist and author of *The Slow Down Diet* and *Nourishing Wisdom: A Mind-Body Approach to Nutrition and Well-Being*.

Zen Master Eihei Dogen (1200–1253) was the founder of the Soto School of Zen and among the first teachers to transmit Zen Buddhism from China to Japan.

Johannes Eckhart, more commonly known as Meister Eckhart (1260–1327), was a member of the Dominican Order and taught all over Europe. He was one of the great speculative mystics who sought to reconcile traditional Christian beliefs with the transcendental metaphysics of Neo-Platonism.

Marcia Falk is a poet, translator, and Judaic scholar. She is the author of *The Book of Blessings: New Jewish Prayers for Daily Life, the Sabbath, and the New Moon Festival; The Song of Songs: Love Lyrics from the Bible*; and two books of her own poetry, *It Is July in Virginia* and *My Son Likes Weather.*

Rick Fields (1942–1999) was a respected journalist and leading authority on American Buddhism. He published several books, including *How the Swans Came to the Lake* and is coauthor of *Instructions to the Cook.*

Betty Fussell is the author of nine books, including *I Hear America Cooking* and *My Kitchen Wars.*

Kahlil Gibran (1883–1931) was an artist, a poet, and a writer. His books include *The Prophet, Sand and Foam, The Earth Gods,* and *The Wanderer.*

Father John Giuliani is an internationally exhibited artist whose works blend Native American images with Christian iconography. He oversees the Benedictine Grange in West Redding, Connecticut, which he founded in 1977.

Bernard Glassman is the abbot of the Zen Community of New York and also the Zen Center of Los Angeles. He is a former aerospace engineer, the cofounder of the Zen Peacemaker Order, and author or coauthor of several books, including *Instructions to the Cook.*

Jane Goodall is the world's foremost authority on chimpanzees. An internationally renowned conservationist, she is the founder of the Jane Goodall Institute and has received many distinguished awards in science. Dr. Goodall is also the author of many acclaimed books, including *Reason for Hope.*

Joan Halifax Roshi is a Buddhist teacher, Zen priest, anthropologist, and author. She is founder, abbot, and head teacher of Upaya Zen Center, a Buddhist monastery in Santa Fe, New Mexico. A founding teacher of the Zen Peacemaker Order, her work and practice for more than three decades has focused on engaged Buddhism.

Thich Nhat Hanh, a Buddhist monk since the age of sixteen, has been living in exile from his Vietnamese homeland for more than thirty years. He is a noted advocate of peace and has written more than seventy-five books of prose, poetry, and prayers.

Julia S. Kasdorf's books of poetry include *Eve's Striptease* and *Sleeping Preacher,* which received the 1991 Agnes Lynch Starrett Poetry Prize and the Great Lakes Colleges Award for New Writing in 1993.

Karyn D. Kedar teaches matters of the spirit to groups throughout the United States. She is senior rabbi at Congregation B'nai Jehoshua Beth Elohim in the Chicago area, and the author of several books, including *The Bridge to Forgiveness: Stories and Prayers for Finding God and Restoring Wholeness; Our Dance with God: Finding Prayer, Perspective and Meaning in the Stories of Our Lives*; and *God Whispers: Stories of the Soul, Lessons of the Heart* (all Jewish Lights).

Haven Kimmel is the author of several books including *The Used World* and *A Girl Named Zippy*. She studied literature and creative writing at Ball State University and North Carolina State University, and also attended seminary at the Earlham School of Religion.

Barbara Kingsolver is the author of ten books, including *Small Wonder* and *Animal, Vegetable, Miracle*. In 2000 she was awarded the National Humanities Medal for service through the arts. She lives with her husband and two daughters on a farm in southern Appalachia.

Jacqueline Kramer is the author of *Buddha Mom: The Path of Mindful Mothering and Spiritual Practices for Busy Parents*. She is the founder of the Hearth Foundation, a non-profit organization dedicated to supporting home-based spiritual practice through information sharing and community building.

Rabbi Irwin Kula is the coeditor with Vanessa L. Ochs of *The Book of Jewish Sacred Practices: CLAL's Guide to Everyday & Holiday Rituals & Blessings* (Jewish Lights).

Brother Lawrence (Nicholas Herman, c. 1605–1691) was born in Lorraine province, France. After serving as a soldier and a footman, he entered the religious community of the Carmelites, where he worked in the kitchen. His writings were edited after his death by Abbe de Beautfort and printed in two volumes: *Maximes Spirituelles* and *Moeurs et Entretiens du Frère Laurent*.

Julius Lester has published thirty-five books of fiction, nonfiction, and poetry, as well as children's books, including *Lovesong: Becoming a Jew*. His work has received the Newbery Honor, the Lewis Carroll Shelf Award, and the Boston Globe/Horn Book Award.

Alison Luterman is a poet, essayist, and playwright who blogs about art, life, performance, and poetry at www.seehowwealmostfly.blogspot.com. She lives in Oakland, California.

Sister Miriam Therese MacGillis is a member of the Dominican Sisters of Caldwell, New Jersey. She is the director of Genesis Farm, which she cofounded in 1980 with the sponsorship of her Dominican congregation. Genesis Farm is a learning center for earth studies.

J. B. MacKinnon is the coauthor of *Plenty: One Man, One Woman, and a Raucous Year of Eating Locally*. He is the author of *Dead Man in Paradise* in addition to award-winning magazine pieces and a former senior editor at *Adbusters*. He lives in Vancouver.

Sara Miles is the author of *Take This Bread* and *How to Hack a Party Line: The Democrats and Silicon Valley*. Her work has appeared in numerous national magazines. She is the founder of St. Gregory's Food Pantry in San Francisco.

Helen Nearing has authored or coauthored twelve books including *Living the Good Life, Continuing the Good Life,* and *The Maple Sugar Book.*

Kent Nerburn is the highly acclaimed author of eight books on spiritual values and Native American themes including *Simple Truths; Small Graces; Make Me an Instrument of Your Peace; A Haunting Reverence; Letters to My Son;* and *Neither Wolf nor Dog: On Forgotten Roads with an Indian Elder.* His most recent work is *Chief Joseph and the Flight of the Nez Perce: The Untold Story of an American Tragedy.*

Bich Minh Nguyen is the author of *Stealing Buddha's Dinner*, which was awarded the PEN/Jerard Fund Award. She teaches literature and creative writing at Purdue University.

Vanessa L. Ochs is a recipient of a fellowship in creative writing from the National Endowment of the Arts. She is author of several books and coeditor, with Rabbi Irwin Kula, of *The Book of Jewish Sacred Practices: CLAL's Guide to Everyday & Holiday Rituals & Blessings.*

Mary Oliver is a winner of the Pulitzer Prize for poetry. Her books include *Blue Iris, Why I Wake Early, Owls and Other Fantasies, White Pine, West Wind, The Leaf and the Cloud,* and *What Do We Know,* as well as five books of prose, including *Rules for the Dance.*

Mary Rose O'Reilley is the author of *The Barn at the End of the World; The Love of Impermanent Things;* and the Walt Whitman Award–winning *Half Wild: Poems.*

Grace Paley (1922–2007) was the author of three highly acclaimed collections of short fiction—*The Little Disturbances of Man, Enormous Changes at the Last Minute,* and *Later the Same Day*—as well as three collections of poetry. She was a member of the War Resister League, RESIST, Women's Pentagon Action, and a founder of the Greenwich Village Peace Center.

Lawrence Raab is the author of six collections of poetry, including *The Probable World; What We Don't Know about Each Other,* a winner of the National Poetry Series and a finalist for the National Book Award; and *Visible Signs: New and Selected Poems.*

Jalal ad-Din ar-Rumi (c. 1207–1273) was a great Islamic Persian sage and poet mystic. His major work was the *Mathnawi*, six volumes of spiritual teaching and Sufi lore in the form of stories and lyric poetry.

Omid Safi is the cochair of the steering committee for the study of Islam at the American Academy of Religion and an assistant professor of Islamic studies at Colgate University. He is the editor of *Progressive Muslims: On Justice, Gender, and Pluralism* and the author of *The Politics of Knowledge in Premodern Islam.*

Rabbi Zalman M. Schachter-Shalomi, professor emeritus at Temple University, is also on the faculty of religious studies at Naropa University. He is the author of *First Steps to a New Jewish Spirit: Reb Zalman's Guide to Recapturing the*

Intimacy & Ecstacy in Your Relationship with God (Jewish Lights) and *Wrapped in a Holy Flame*.

Lynne Meredith Schreiber is from Southfield, Michigan, where she lives with her three amazing children and writes about how people find meaning in the mundane. Her work has appeared in *Saveur, Better Homes and Gardens, AARP,* and the *Chicago Tribune*. She has written six books, including *Hide and Seek: Jewish Women and Hair Covering*.

Rabbi Rami Shapiro is an award-winning storyteller, poet, and essayist, and director of the Simply Jewish Foundation. He is the author of *Minyan: Ten Principles for Living a Life of Integrity*. He is the author, translator, and annotator of several books, including *Ethics of the Sages: Pirke Avot—Annotated & Explained; Hasidic Tales: Annotated & Explained; The Hebrew Prophets: Selections Annotated & Explained; The Divine Feminine in Biblical Wisdom Literature: Selections Annotated & Explained;* and *The Sacred Art of Lovingkindness: Preparing to Practice* (all SkyLight Paths).

Guru Gobind Singh (1666–1708) was the tenth Guru of the Sikhs, a scholar, and a military hero. The *Adi Granth* (the scripture of the Sikhs) took its final form under the supervision of Gobind Singh, as did the *Dasam Granth*, a collection of prayers, poetry, and narrative.

Alisa Smith is the coauthor of *Plenty: One Man, One Woman, and a Raucous Year of Eating Locally*. Her writing has appeared in *Utne Reader, Reader's Digest, Outside*, and many other publications. She lives in Vancouver.

Daisetz Teitaro Suzuki (1870–1966), Japanese Buddhist scholar, was a leading authority on Buddhism and is known for his introduction of Zen Buddhism to the West. Among his many works are *Essays in Zen Buddhism, The Training of the Zen Buddhist Monk, Zen Buddhism and Its Influence on Japanese Culture,* and *Mysticism: Christian and Buddhist*.

Jessica Swift is a writer and editor living in Vermont.

Nancy Willard is the author of two novels, *Things Invisible to See* and *Sister Water*, and eleven books of poetry, including *Water Walker* and *In the Salt Marsh*. She has been awarded grants from the National Endowment for the Arts in both fiction and poetry, and her book *A Visit to William Blake's Inn* was awarded the Newbery Medal.

Kristen Wolf is an author, filmmaker, and small business owner living in California, where she's earning her pilot's license and completing her first novel.

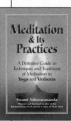

Children's Spirituality

Adam and Eve's First Sunset: God's New Day
by Sandy Eisenberg Sasso; Full-color illus. by Joani Keller Rothenberg
9 x 12, 32 pp, Full-color illus., HC, 978-1-58023-177-0 **$17.95** *For ages 4 & up (a Jewish Lights book)*

Because Nothing Looks Like God
by Lawrence and Karen Kushner; Full-color illus. by Dawn W. Majewski
Real-life examples of happiness and sadness introduce children to the possibilities of spiritual life. 11 x 8½, 32 pp, HC, Full-color illus., 978-1-58023-092-6 **$17.99** *For ages 4 & up (a Jewish Lights book)*

Also available: **Teacher's Guide,** 8½ x 11, 22 pp, PB, 978-1-58023-140-4 **$6.95** *For ages 5–8*

Becoming Me: A Story of Creation
by Martin Boroson; Full-color illus. by Christopher Gilvan-Cartwright
Told in the personal "voice" of the Creator, a story about creation and relationship that is about each one of us.
8 x 10, 32 pp, Full-color illus., HC, 978-1-893361-11-9 **$16.95** *For ages 4 & up*

But God Remembered: Stories of Women from Creation to the Promised Land   *by Sandy Eisenberg Sasso; Full-color illus. by Bethanne Andersen*
A fascinating collection of four different stories of women only briefly mentioned in biblical tradition and religious texts. 9 x 12, 32 pp, HC, Full-color illus., 978-1-879045-43-9 **$16.95** *For ages 8 & up (a Jewish Lights book)*

Cain & Abel: Finding the Fruits of Peace
by Sandy Eisenberg Sasso; Full-color illus. by Joani Keller Rothenberg
A sensitive recasting of the ancient tale shows we have the power to deal with anger in positive ways. "Editor's Choice"—American Library Association's *Booklist*
9 x 12, 32 pp, HC, Full-color illus., 978-1-58023-123-7 **$16.95** *For ages 5 & up (a Jewish Lights book)*

Does God Hear My Prayer?
by August Gold; Full-color photos by Diane Hardy Waller
Introduces preschoolers and young readers to prayer and how it helps them express their own emotions. 10 x 8½, 32 pp, Quality PB, Full-color photo illus., 978-1-59473-102-0 **$8.99**

The 11th Commandment: Wisdom from Our Children *by The Children of America*
"If there were an Eleventh Commandment, what would it be?" Children of many religious denominations across America answer this question—in their own drawings and words. "A rare book of spiritual celebration for all people, of all ages, for all time." —*Bookviews*
8 x 10, 48 pp, HC, Full-color illus., 978-1-879045-46-0 **$16.95** *For all ages (a Jewish Lights book)*

For Heaven's Sake *by Sandy Eisenberg Sasso; Full-color illus. by Kathryn Kunz Finney*
Everyone talked about heaven: "Thank heavens." "Heaven forbid." "For heaven's sake, Isaiah." But no one would say what heaven was or how to find it. So Isaiah decides to find out, by seeking answers from many different people.
9 x 12, 32 pp, HC, Full-color illus., 978-1-58023-054-4 **$16.95** *For ages 4 & up (a Jewish Lights book)*

God in Between *by Sandy Eisenberg Sasso; Full-color illus. by Sally Sweetland*
A magical, mythical tale that teaches that God can be found where we are.
9 x 12, 32 pp, HC, Full-color illus., 978-1-879045-86-6 **$16.95** *For ages 4 & up (a Jewish Lights book)*

God's Paintbrush: Special 10th Anniversary Edition
Invites children of all faiths and backgrounds to encounter God through moments in their own lives. 11 x 8½, 32 pp, Full-color illus., HC, 978-1-58023-195-4 **$17.95** *For ages 4 & up*

Also available: **God's Paintbrush Teacher's Guide** 8½ x 11, 32 pp, PB, 978-1-879045-57-6 **$8.95**

God's Paintbrush Celebration Kit
A Spiritual Activity Kit for Teachers and Students of All Faiths, All Backgrounds
Additional activity sheets available:
8-Student Activity Sheet Pack (40 sheets/5 sessions), 978-1-58023-058-2 **$19.95**
Single-Student Activity Sheet Pack (5 sessions), 978-1-58023-059-9 **$3.95**

Midrash Fiction / Folktales

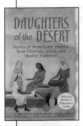

Abraham's Bind & Other Bible Tales of Trickery, Folly, Mercy and Love   by Michael J. Caduto

New retellings of episodes in the lives of familiar biblical characters explore relevant life lessons.

6 x 9, 224 pp, HC, 978-1-59473-186-0 **$19.99**

Daughters of the Desert: Stories of Remarkable Women from Christian, Jewish and Muslim Traditions   by Claire Rudolf Murphy, Meghan Nuttall Sayres, Mary Cronk Farrell, Sarah Conover and Betsy Wharton

Breathes new life into the old tales of our female ancestors in faith. Uses traditional scriptural passages as starting points, then with vivid detail fills in historical context and place. Chapters reveal the voices of Sarah, Hagar, Huldah, Esther, Salome, Mary Magdalene, Lydia, Khadija, Fatima and many more. Historical fiction ideal for readers of all ages. Quality paperback includes reader's discussion guide.

5½ x 8½, 192 pp, Quality PB, 978-1-59473-106-8 **$14.99**
HC, 192 pp, 978-1-893361-72-0 **$19.95**

The Triumph of Eve & Other Subversive Bible Tales
by Matt Biers-Ariel

Many people were taught and remember only a one-dimensional Bible. These engaging retellings are the antidote to this—they're witty, often hilarious, always profound, and invite you to grapple with questions and issues that are often hidden in the original text.

5½ x 8½, 192 pp, Quality PB, 978-1-59473-176-1 **$14.99**

Also avail.: **The Triumph of Eve Teacher's Guide**
8½ x 11, 44 pp, PB, 978-1-59473-152-5 **$8.99**

Wisdom in the Telling
Finding Inspiration and Grace in Traditional Folktales and Myths Retold
by Lorraine Hartin-Gelardi
6 x 9, 224 pp, HC, 978-1-59473-185-3 **$19.99**

Religious Etiquette / Reference

How to Be a Perfect Stranger, 4th Edition: The Essential Religious Etiquette Handbook   Edited by Stuart M. Matlins and Arthur J. Magida

The indispensable guidebook to help the well-meaning guest when visiting other people's religious ceremonies. A straightforward guide to the rituals and celebrations of the major religions and denominations in the United States and Canada from the perspective of an interested guest of any other faith, based on information obtained from authorities of each religion. Belongs in every living room, library and office. Covers:

African American Methodist Churches • Assemblies of God • Bahá'í • Baptist • Buddhist • Christian Church (Disciples of Christ) • Christian Science (Church of Christ, Scientist) • Churches of Christ • Episcopalian and Anglican • Hindu • Islam • Jehovah's Witnesses • Jewish • Lutheran • Mennonite/Amish • Methodist • Mormon (Church of Jesus Christ of Latter-day Saints) • Native American/First Nations • Orthodox Churches • Pentecostal Church of God • Presbyterian • Quaker (Religious Society of Friends) • Reformed Church in America/Canada • Roman Catholic • Seventh-day Adventist • Sikh • Unitarian Universalist • United Church of Canada • United Church of Christ

6 x 9, 432 pp, Quality PB, 978-1-59473-140-2 **$19.99**

The Perfect Stranger's Guide to Funerals and Grieving Practices: A Guide to Etiquette in Other People's Religious Ceremonies   Edited by Stuart M. Matlins
6 x 9, 240 pp, Quality PB, 978-1-893361-20-1 **$16.95**

The Perfect Stranger's Guide to Wedding Ceremonies: A Guide to Etiquette in Other People's Religious Ceremonies   Edited by Stuart M. Matlins
6 x 9, 208 pp, Quality PB, 978-1-893361-19-5 **$16.95**

Sacred Texts—SkyLight Illuminations Series

Offers today's spiritual seeker an accessible entry into the great classic texts of the world's spiritual traditions. Each classic is presented in an accessible translation, with facing pages of guided commentary from experts, giving you the keys you need to understand the history, context and meaning of the text. This series enables you, whatever your background, to experience and understand classic spiritual texts directly, and to make them a part of your life.

CHRISTIANITY

The End of Days: Essential Selections from Apocalyptic Texts—
Annotated & Explained *Annotation by Robert G. Clouse*
Helps you understand the complex Christian visions of the end of the world.
5½ x 8½, 224 pp, Quality PB, 978-1-59473-170-9 **$16.99**

The Hidden Gospel of Matthew: Annotated & Explained
Translation & Annotation by Ron Miller
Takes you deep into the text cherished around the world to discover the words and events that have the strongest connection to the historical Jesus.
5½ x 8½, 272 pp, Quality PB, 978-1-59473-038-2 **$16.99**

The Lost Sayings of Jesus: Teachings from Ancient Christian, Jewish,
Gnostic and Islamic Sources—Annotated & Explained
Translation & Annotation by Andrew Phillip Smith; Foreword by Stephan A. Hoeller
This collection of more than three hundred sayings depicts Jesus as a Wisdom teacher who speaks to people of all faiths as a mystic and spiritual master.
5½ x 8½, 240 pp, Quality PB, 978-1-59473-172-3 **$16.99**

Philokalia: The Eastern Christian Spiritual Texts—Selections Annotated &
Explained *Annotation by Allyne Smith; Translation by G. E. H. Palmer, Phillip Sherrard and Bishop Kallistos Ware*
The first approachable introduction to the wisdom of the Philokalia, which is the classic text of Eastern Christian spirituality.
5½ x 8½, 240 pp, Quality PB, 978-1-59473-103-7 **$16.99**

The Sacred Writings of Paul: Selections Annotated & Explained
Translation & Annotation by Ron Miller
Explores the apostle Paul's core message of spiritual equality, freedom and joy.
5½ x 8½, 224 pp, Quality PB, 978-1-59473-213-3 **$16.99**

Sex Texts from the Bible: Selections Annotated & Explained
Translation & Annotation by Teresa J. Hornsby; Foreword by Amy-Jill Levine
Offers surprising insight into our modern sexual lives.
5½ x 8½, 208 pp, Quality PB, 978-1-59473-217-1 **$16.99**

Spiritual Writings on Mary: Annotated & Explained
Annotation by Mary Ford-Grabowsky; Foreword by Andrew Harvey
Examines the role of Mary, the mother of Jesus, as a source of inspiration in history and in life today. 5½ x 8½, 288 pp, Quality PB, 978-1-59473-001-6 **$16.99**

The Way of a Pilgrim: The Jesus Prayer Journey—Annotated & Explained
Translation & Annotation by Gleb Pokrovsky; Foreword by Andrew Harvey
This classic of Russian spirituality is the delightful account of one man who sets out to learn the prayer of the heart, also known as the "Jesus prayer."
5½ x 8½, 160 pp, Illus., Quality PB, 978-1-893361-31-7 **$14.95**

Sacred Texts—cont.

MORMONISM

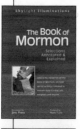

The Book of Mormon: Selections Annotated & Explained
Annotation by Jana Riess; Foreword by Phyllis Tickle
Explores the sacred epic that is cherished by more than twelve million members of the LDS church as the keystone of their faith.
5½ x 8½ , 272 pp, Quality PB, 978-1-59473-076-4 **$16.99**

NATIVE AMERICAN

Native American Stories of the Sacred: Annotated & Explained
Retold & Annotated by Evan T. Pritchard
Intended for more than entertainment, these teaching tales contain elegantly simple illustrations of time-honored truths.
5½ x 8½, 272 pp, Quality PB, 978-1-59473-112-9 **$16.99**

GNOSTICISM

Gnostic Writings on the Soul: Annotated & Explained
Translation & Annotation by Andrew Phillip Smith; Foreword by Stephan A. Hoeller
Reveals the inspiring ways your soul can remember and return to its unique, divine purpose.
5½ x 8½, 144 pp, Quality PB, 978-1-59473-220-1 **$16.99**

The Gospel of Philip: Annotated & Explained
Translation & Annotation by Andrew Phillip Smith; Foreword by Stevan Davies
Reveals otherwise unrecorded sayings of Jesus and fragments of Gnostic mythology.
5½ x 8½, 160 pp, Quality PB, 978-1-59473-111-2 **$16.99**

The Gospel of Thomas: Annotated & Explained
Translation & Annotation by Stevan Davies Sheds new light on the origins of Christianity and portrays Jesus as a wisdom-loving sage.
5½ x 8½, 192 pp, Quality PB, 978-1-893361-45-4 **$16.99**

The Secret Book of John: The Gnostic Gospel—Annotated & Explained
Translation & Annotation by Stevan Davies The most significant and influential text of the ancient Gnostic religion.
5½ x 8½, 208 pp, Quality PB, 978-1-59473-082-5 **$16.99**

JUDAISM

The Divine Feminine in Biblical Wisdom Literature
Selections Annotated & Explained
Translation & Annotation by Rabbi Rami Shapiro; Foreword by Rev. Cynthia Bourgeault, PhD
Uses the Hebrew books of Psalms, Proverbs, Song of Songs, Ecclesiastes and Job, Wisdom literature and the Wisdom of Solomon to clarify who Wisdom is.
5½ x 8½, 240 pp, Quality PB, 978-1-59473-109-9 **$16.99**

Ethics of the Sages: *Pirke Avot*—Annotated & Explained
Translation & Annotation by Rabbi Rami Shapiro Clarifies the ethical teachings of the early Rabbis. 5½ x 8½, 192 pp, Quality PB, 978-1-59473-207-2 **$16.99**

Hasidic Tales: Annotated & Explained
Translation & Annotation by Rabbi Rami Shapiro
Introduces the legendary tales of the impassioned Hasidic rabbis, presenting them as stories rather than as parables. 5½ x 8½, 240 pp, Quality PB, 978-1-893361-86-7 **$16.95**

The Hebrew Prophets: Selections Annotated & Explained
Translation & Annotation by Rabbi Rami Shapiro; Foreword by Zalman M. Schachter-Shalomi
Focuses on the central themes covered by all the Hebrew prophets.
5½ x 8½, 224 pp, Quality PB, 978-1-59473-037-5 **$16.99**

Zohar: Annotated & Explained *Translation & Annotation by Daniel C. Matt*
The best-selling author of *The Essential Kabbalah* brings together in one place the most important teachings of the Zohar, the canonical text of Jewish mystical tradition.
5½ x 8½, 176 pp, Quality PB, 978-1-893361-51-5 **$15.99**

Sacred Texts—cont.

ISLAM

The Qur'an and Sayings of Prophet Muhammad
Selections Annotated & Explained
Annotation by Sohaib N. Sultan; Translation by Yusuf Ali; Revised by Sohaib N. Sultan
Foreword by Jane I. Smith
Explores how the timeless wisdom of the Qur'an can enrich your own spiritual journey.
5½ x 8½, 256 pp, Quality PB, 978-1-59473-222-5 **$16.99**

Rumi and Islam: Selections from His Stories, Poems, and Discourses—Annotated & Explained
Translation & Annotation by Ibrahim Gamard
Focuses on Rumi's place within the Sufi tradition of Islam, providing insight into the mystical side of the religion.
5½ x 8½, 240 pp, Quality PB, 978-1-59473-002-3 **$15.99**

EASTERN RELIGIONS

The Art of War—Spirituality for Conflict
Annotated & Explained
by Sun Tzu; Annotation by Thomas Huynh; Translation by Thomas Huynh and the Editors at Sonshi.com; Foreword by Marc Benioff; Preface by Thomas Cleary
Highlights principles that encourage a perceptive and spiritual approach to conflict.
5½ x 8½, 256 pp, Quality PB, 978-1-59473-244-7 **$16.99**

Bhagavad Gita: Annotated & Explained
Translation by Shri Purohit Swami; Annotation by Kendra Crossen Burroughs
Explains references and philosophical terms, shares the interpretations of famous spiritual leaders and scholars, and more.
5½ x 8½, 192 pp, Quality PB, 978-1-893361-28-7 **$16.95**

Dhammapada: Annotated & Explained
Translation by Max Müller and revised by Jack Maguire; Annotation by Jack Maguire
Contains all of Buddhism's key teachings.
5½ x 8½, 160 pp, b/w photos, Quality PB, 978-1-893361-42-3 **$14.95**

Selections from the Gospel of Sri Ramakrishna
Annotated & Explained
Translation by Swami Nikhilananda; Annotation by Kendra Crossen Burroughs
Introduces the fascinating world of the Indian mystic and the universal appeal of his message.
5½ x 8½, 240 pp, b/w photos, Quality PB, 978-1-893361-46-1 **$16.95**

Tao Te Ching: Annotated & Explained
Translation & Annotation by Derek Lin; Foreword by Lama Surya Das
Introduces an Eastern classic in an accessible, poetic and completely original way.
5½ x 8½, 192 pp, Quality PB, 978-1-59473-204-1 **$16.99**

STOICISM

The Meditations of Marcus Aurelius
Selections Annotated & Explained
Annotation by Russell McNeil, PhD; Translation by George Long; Revised by Russell McNeil, PhD
Offers insightful and engaging commentary into the historical background of Stoicism.
5½ x 8½, 288 pp, Quality PB, 978-1-59473-236-2 **$16.99**

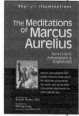

Spiritual Biography / Reference

Spiritual Leaders Who Changed the World
The Essential Handbook to the Past Century of Religion
Edited by Ira Rifkin and the Editors at SkyLight Paths; Foreword by Dr. Robert Coles
An invaluable reference to the most important spiritual leaders of the past 100 years.
6 x 9, 304 pp, 15+ b/w photos, Quality PB, 978-1-59473-241-6 **$18.99**

Spiritual Biography—SkyLight Lives

SkyLight Lives reintroduces the lives and works of key spiritual figures of our time—people who by their teaching or example have challenged our assumptions about spirituality and have caused us to look at it in new ways.

The Life of Evelyn Underhill
An Intimate Portrait of the Groundbreaking Author of Mysticism
by Margaret Cropper; Foreword by Dana Greene
Evelyn Underhill was a passionate writer and teacher who wrote elegantly on mysticism, worship, and devotional life.
6 x 9, 288 pp, 5 b/w photos, Quality PB, 978-1-893361-70-6 **$18.95**

Mahatma Gandhi: His Life and Ideas
by Charles F. Andrews; Foreword by Dr. Arun Gandhi
Examines from a contemporary Christian activist's point of view the religious ideas and political dynamics that influenced the birth of the peaceful resistance movement.
6 x 9, 336 pp, 5 b/w photos, Quality PB, 978-1-893361-89-8 **$18.95**

Simone Weil: A Modern Pilgrimage
by Robert Coles
The extraordinary life of the spiritual philosopher who's been called both saint and madwoman.
6 x 9, 208 pp, Quality PB, 978-1-893361-34-8 **$16.95**

Zen Effects: The Life of Alan Watts
by Monica Furlong
Through his widely popular books and lectures, Alan Watts (1915–1973) did more to introduce Eastern philosophy and religion to Western minds than any figure before or since.
6 x 9, 264 pp, Quality PB, 978-1-893361-32-4 **$16.95**

More Spiritual Biography

Bede Griffiths: An Introduction to His Interspiritual Thought
by Wayne Teasdale
The first study of his contemplative experience and thought, exploring the intersection of Hinduism and Christianity.
6 x 9, 288 pp, Quality PB, 978-1-893361-77-5 **$18.95**

The Soul of the Story: Meetings with Remarkable People
by Rabbi David Zeller
Inspiring and entertaining, this compelling collection of spiritual adventures assures us that no spiritual lesson truly learned is ever lost.
6 x 9, 288 pp, HC, 978-1-58023-272-2 **$21.99** *(a Jewish Lights book)*

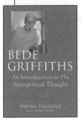

Spiritual Poetry—The Mystic Poets

Experience these mystic poets as you never have before. Each beautiful, compact book includes: a brief introduction to the poet's time and place; a summary of the major themes of the poet's mysticism and religious tradition; essential selections from the poet's most important works; and an appreciative preface by a contemporary spiritual writer.

Hafiz
The Mystic Poets
Preface by Ibrahim Gamard

Hafiz is known throughout the world as Persia's greatest poet, with sales of his poems in Iran today only surpassed by those of the Qur'an itself. His probing and joyful verse speaks to people from all backgrounds who long to taste and feel divine love and experience harmony with all living things.

5 x 7¼, 144 pp, HC, 978-1-59473-009-2 **$16.99**

Hopkins
The Mystic Poets
Preface by Rev. Thomas Ryan, CSP

Gerard Manley Hopkins, Christian mystical poet, is beloved for his use of fresh language and startling metaphors to describe the world around him. Although his verse is lovely, beneath the surface lies a searching soul, wrestling with and yearning for God.

5 x 7¼, 112 pp, HC, 978-1-59473-010-8 **$16.99**

Tagore
The Mystic Poets
Preface by Swami Adiswarananda

Rabindranath Tagore is often considered the "Shakespeare" of modern India. A great mystic, Tagore was the teacher of W. B. Yeats and Robert Frost, the close friend of Albert Einstein and Mahatma Gandhi, and the winner of the Nobel Prize for Literature. This beautiful sampling of Tagore's two most important works, *The Gardener* and *Gitanjali,* offers a glimpse into his spiritual vision that has inspired people around the world.

5 x 7¼, 144 pp, HC, 978-1-59473-008-5 **$16.99**

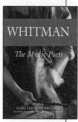

Whitman
The Mystic Poets
Preface by Gary David Comstock

Walt Whitman was the most innovative and influential poet of the nineteenth century. This beautiful sampling of Whitman's most important poetry from *Leaves of Grass*, and selections from his prose writings, offers a glimpse into the spiritual side of his most radical themes—love for country, love for others, and love of Self.

5 x 7¼, 192 pp, HC, 978-1-59473-041-2 **$16.99**

Journeys of Simplicity
Traveling Light with Thomas Merton, Bashō, Edward Abbey, Annie Dillard & Others

Invites you to consider a more graceful way of traveling through life. Use the included journal pages (in PB only) to help you get started on your own spiritual journey.

Ed. by Philip Harnden

5 x 7¼, 144 pp, Quality PB, 978-1-59473-181-5 **$12.99**

128 pp, HC, 978-1-893361-76-8 **$16.95**

Spirituality of the Seasons

Autumn: A Spiritual Biography of the Season
Edited by Gary Schmidt and Susan M. Felch; Illustrations by Mary Azarian
Rejoice in autumn as a time of preparation and reflection. Includes Wendell Berry, David James Duncan, Robert Frost, A. Bartlett Giamatti, E. B. White, P. D. James, Julian of Norwich, Garret Keizer, Tracy Kidder, Anne Lamott, May Sarton.
6 x 9, 320 pp, 5 b/w illus., Quality PB, 978-1-59473-118-1 **$18.99**

Spring: A Spiritual Biography of the Season
Edited by Gary Schmidt and Susan M. Felch; Illustrations by Mary Azarian
Explore the gentle unfurling of spring and reflect on how nature celebrates rebirth and renewal. Includes Jane Kenyon, Lucy Larcom, Harry Thurston, Nathaniel Hawthorne, Noel Perrin, Annie Dillard, Martha Ballard, Barbara Kingsolver, Dorothy Wordsworth, Donald Hall, David Brill, Lionel Basney, Isak Dinesen, Paul Laurence Dunbar. 6 x 9, 352 pp, 6 b/w illus., Quality PB, 978-1-59473-246-1 **$18.99**

Summer: A Spiritual Biography of the Season
Edited by Gary Schmidt and Susan M. Felch; Illustrations by Barry Moser
"A sumptuous banquet.... These selections lift up an exquisite wholeness found within an everyday sophistication."— ★ *Publishers Weekly* starred review
Includes Anne Lamott, Luci Shaw, Ray Bradbury, Richard Selzer, Thomas Lynch, Walt Whitman, Carl Sandburg, Sherman Alexie, Madeleine L'Engle, Jamaica Kincaid.
6 x 9, 304 pp, 5 b/w illus., Quality PB, 978-1-59473-183-9 **$18.99**
HC, 978-1-59473-083-2 **$21.99**

Winter: A Spiritual Biography of the Season
Edited by Gary Schmidt and Susan M. Felch; Illustrations by Barry Moser
"This outstanding anthology features top-flight nature and spirituality writers on the fierce, inexorable season of winter.... Remarkably lively and warm, despite the icy subject." — ★ *Publishers Weekly* starred review
Includes Will Campbell, Rachel Carson, Annie Dillard, Donald Hall, Ron Hansen, Jane Kenyon, Jamaica Kincaid, Barry Lopez, Kathleen Norris, John Updike, E. B. White.
6 x 9, 288 pp, 6 b/w illus., Deluxe PB w/flaps, 978-1-893361-92-8 **$18.95**
HC, 978-1-893361-53-9 **$21.95**

Spirituality / Animal Companions

Blessing the Animals: Prayers and Ceremonies to Celebrate God's Creatures, Wild and Tame *Edited by Lynn L. Caruso* 5 x 7¼, 256 pp, HC, 978-1-59473-145-7 **$19.99**

Remembering My Pet: A Kid's Own Spiritual Workbook for When a Pet Dies
by Nechama Liss-Levinson, PhD, and Rev. Molly Phinney Baskette, MDiv; Foreword by Lynn L. Caruso
8 x 10, 48 pp, 2-color text, HC, 978-1-59473-221-3 **$16.99**

What Animals Can Teach Us about Spirituality: Inspiring Lessons from Wild and Tame Creatures *by Diana L. Guerrero* 6 x 9, 176 pp, Quality PB, 978-1-893361-84-3 **$16.95**

Spirituality—A Week Inside

Come and Sit: A Week Inside Meditation Centers
by Marcia Z. Nelson; Foreword by Wayne Teasdale
6 x 9, 224 pp, b/w photos, Quality PB, 978-1-893361-35-5 **$16.95**

Lighting the Lamp of Wisdom: A Week Inside a Yoga Ashram
by John Ittner; Foreword by Dr. David Frawley
6 x 9, 192 pp, 10+ b/w photos, Quality PB, 978-1-893361-52-2 **$15.95**

Making a Heart for God: A Week Inside a Catholic Monastery
by Dianne Aprile; Foreword by Brother Patrick Hart, OCSO
6 x 9, 224 pp, b/w photos, Quality PB, 978-1-893361-49-2 **$16.95**

Waking Up: A Week Inside a Zen Monastery
by Jack Maguire; Foreword by John Daido Loori, Roshi
6 x 9, 224 pp, b/w photos, Quality PB, 978-1-893361-55-3 **$16.95**; HC, 978-1-893361-13-3 **$21.95**

Spirituality

Next to Godliness: Finding the Sacred in Housekeeping
Edited and with Introductions by Alice Peck
Offers new perspectives on how we can reach out for the Divine.
6 x 9, 224 pp, Quality PB, 978-1-59473-214-0 **$19.99**

Bread, Body, Spirit: Finding the Sacred in Food
Edited and with Introductions by Alice Peck
Explores how food feeds our faith. 6 x 9, 224 pp, Quality PB, 978-1-59473-242-3 **$19.99**

Renewal in the Wilderness: A Spiritual Guide to Connecting with God
in the Natural World *by John Lionberger*
Reveals the power of experiencing God's presence in many variations of the natural world. 6 x 9, 176 pp, b/w photos, Quality PB, 978-1-59473-219-5 **$16.99**

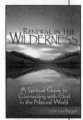

Honoring Motherhood: Prayers, Ceremonies and Blessings
Edited and with Introductions by Lynn L. Caruso
Journey through the seasons of motherhood. 5 x 7¼, 272 pp, HC, 978-1-59473-239-3 **$19.99**

Soul Fire: Accessing Your Creativity *by Rev. Thomas Ryan, CSP*
Learn to cultivate your creative spirit. 6 x 9, 160 pp, Quality PB, 978-1-59473-243-0 **$16.99**

Technology & Spirituality: How the Information Revolution Affects
Our Spiritual Lives *by Stephen K. Spyker* 6 x 9, 176 pp, HC, 978-1-59473-218-8 **$19.99**

Money and the Way of Wisdom: Insights from the Book of Proverbs
by Timothy J. Sandoval, PhD 6 x 9, 192 pp (est), Quality PB, 978-1-59473-245-4 **$16.99**

Awakening the Spirit, Inspiring the Soul
30 Stories of Interspiritual Discovery in the Community of Faiths
Edited by Brother Wayne Teasdale and Martha Howard, MD; Foreword by Joan Borysenko, PhD
6 x 9, 224 pp, HC, 978-1-59473-039-9 **$21.99**

Creating a Spiritual Retirement: A Guide to the Unseen Possibilities in Our Lives
by Molly Srode 6 x 9, 208 pp, b/w photos, Quality PB, 978-1-59473-050-4 **$14.99**
HC, 978-1-893361-75-1 **$19.95**

Finding Hope: Cultivating God's Gift of a Hopeful Spirit
by Marcia Ford 8 x 8, 200 pp, Quality PB, 978-1-59473-211-9 **$16.99**

The Geography of Faith: Underground Conversations on Religious, Political and Social
Change *by Daniel Berrigan and Robert Coles* 6 x 9, 224 pp, Quality PB, 978-1-893361-40-9 **$16.95**

Jewish Spirituality: A Brief Introduction for Christians *by Lawrence Kushner*
5½ x 8½, 112 pp, Quality PB, 978-1-58023-150-3 **$12.95** *(a Jewish Lights book)*

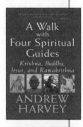

Journeys of Simplicity: Traveling Light with Thomas Merton, Bashō, Edward
Abbey, Annie Dillard & Others *by Philip Harnden* 5 x 7¼, 144 pp, Quality PB, 978-1-59473-
181-5 **$12.99** 128 pp, HC, 978-1-893361-76-8 **$16.95**

Keeping Spiritual Balance As We Grow Older: More than 65 Creative Ways to
Use Purpose, Prayer, and the Power of Spirit to Build a Meaningful Retirement
by Molly and Bernie Srode 8 x 8, 224 pp, Quality PB, 978-1-59473-042-9 **$16.99**

Spirituality 101: The Indispensable Guide to Keeping—or Finding—Your Spiritual Life
on Campus *by Harriet L. Schwartz, with contributions from college students at nearly thirty campuses across the United States* 6 x 9, 272 pp, Quality PB, 978-1-59473-000-9 **$16.99**

Spiritually Incorrect: Finding God in All the Wrong Places *by Dan Wakefield; Illus. by
Marian DelVecchio* 5½ x 8½, 192 pp, b/w illus., Quality PB, 978-1-59473-137-2 **$15.99**

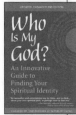

Spiritual Manifestos: Visions for Renewed Religious Life in America from Young
Spiritual Leaders of Many Faiths *Edited by Niles Elliot Goldstein; Preface by Martin E. Marty*
6 x 9, 256 pp, HC, 978-1-893361-09-6 **$21.95**

A Walk with Four Spiritual Guides: Krishna, Buddha, Jesus, and Ramakrishna
by Andrew Harvey 5½ x 8½, 192 pp, 10 b/w photos & illus., Quality PB, 978-1-59473-138-9 **$15.99**

What Matters: Spiritual Nourishment for Head and Heart
by Frederick Franck 5 x 7¼, 128 pp, 50+ b/w illus., HC, 978-1-59473-013-9 **$16.99**

Who Is My God?, 2nd Edition: An Innovative Guide to Finding Your Spiritual Identity
Created by the Editors at SkyLight Paths 6 x 9, 160 pp, Quality PB, 978-1-59473-014-6 **$15.99**

Spirituality & Crafts

The Knitting Way
A Guide to Spiritual Self-Discovery
by Linda Skolnik and Janice MacDaniels
Examines how you can explore and strengthen your spiritual life through knitting.
7 x 9, 240 pp, Quality PB, b/w photographs, 978-1-59473-079-5 **$16.99**

The Scrapbooking Journey
A Hands-On Guide to Spiritual Discovery
by Cory Richardson-Lauve; Foreword by Stacy Julian
Reveals how this craft can become a practice used to deepen and shape your life.
7 x 9, 176 pp, Quality PB, 8-page full-color insert, plus b/w photographs
978-1-59473-216-4 **$18.99**

The Painting Path
Embodying Spiritual Discovery through Yoga, Brush and Color
by Linda Novick; Foreword by Richard Segalman
Explores the divine connection you can experience through creativity.
7 x 9, 208 pp, 8-page full-color insert, plus b/w photographs
Quality PB, 978-1-59473-226-3 **$18.99**

The Quilting Path
A Guide to Spiritual Discovery through Fabric, Thread and Kabbalah
by Louise Silk
Explores how to cultivate personal growth through quilt making.
7 x 9, 192 pp, Quality PB, b/w photographs and illustrations, 978-1-59473-206-5 **$16.99**

Contemplative Crochet
A Hands-On Guide for Interlocking Faith and Craft
by Cindy Crandall-Frazier; Foreword by Linda Skolnik
Illuminates the spiritual lessons you can learn through crocheting.
7 x 9, 192 pp (est), b/w photographs, Quality PB, 978-1-59473-238-6 **$16.99**

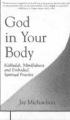

Kabbalah / Enneagram
(from Jewish Lights Publishing)

God in Your Body: Kabbalah, Mindfulness and Embodied Spiritual Practice
by Jay Michaelson 6 x 9, Quality PB Original, 978-1-58023-304-0 **$18.99**

Cast in God's Image: Discover Your Personality Type Using the Enneagram and Kabbalah
by Rabbi Howard A. Addison 7 x 9, 176 pp, Quality PB, 978-1-58023-124-4 **$16.95**

Ehyeh: A Kabbalah for Tomorrow *by Dr. Arthur Green*
6 x 9, 224 pp, Quality PB, 978-1-58023-213-5 **$16.99**

The Enneagram and Kabbalah, 2nd Edition: Reading Your Soul
by Rabbi Howard A. Addison 6 x 9, 192 pp, Quality PB, 978-1-58023-229-6 **$16.99**

The Gift of Kabbalah: Discovering the Secrets of Heaven, Renewing Your Life on Earth
by Tamar Frankiel, PhD 6 x 9, 256 pp, Quality PB, 978-1-58023-141-1 **$16.95**
HC, 978-1-58023-108-4 **$21.95**

Kabbalah: A Brief Introduction for Christians
by Tamar Frankiel, PhD 5½ x 8½, 176 pp, Quality PB, 978-1-58023-303-3 **$16.99**

Zohar: Annotated & Explained *Translation and Annotation by Dr. Daniel C. Matt*
Foreword by Andrew Harvey 5½ x 8½, 176 pp, Quality PB, 978-1-893361-51-5 **$15.99**
(a SkyLight Paths book)

Spiritual Practice

Soul Fire: Accessing Your Creativity *by Rev. Thomas Ryan, CSP*
Shows you how to cultivate your creative spirit as a way to encourage personal growth.
6 x 9, 160 pp, Quality PB, 978-1-59473-243-0 **$16.99**

Running—The Sacred Art: Preparing to Practice
by Dr. Warren A. Kay; Foreword by Kristin Armstrong
Examines how your daily run can enrich your spiritual life.
5½ x 8½, 160 pp, Quality PB, 978-1-59473-227-0 **$16.99**

Hospitality—The Sacred Art: Discovering the Hidden Spiritual Power
of Invitation and Welcome *by Rev. Nanette Sawyer; Foreword by Rev. Dirk Ficca*
Explores how this ancient spiritual practice can transform your relationships.
5½ x 8½, 192 pp, Quality PB, 978-1-59473-228-7 **$16.99**

Thanking & Blessing—The Sacred Art: Spiritual Vitality through
Gratefulness *by Jay Marshall, PhD; Foreword by Philip Gulley*
Offers practical tips for uncovering the blessed wonder in our lives—even in trying circumstances. 5½ x 8½, 176 pp, Quality PB, 978-1-59473-231-7 **$16.99**

Everyday Herbs in Spiritual Life: A Guide to Many Practices
by Michael J. Caduto; Foreword by Rosemary Gladstar Explores the power of herbs.
7 x 9, 208 pp, 21 b/w illustrations, Quality PB, 978-1-59473-174-7 **$16.99**

Divining the Body: Reclaim the Holiness of Your Physical Self *by Jan Phillips*
8 x 8, 256 pp, Quality PB, 978-1-59473-080-1 **$16.99**

Finding Time for the Timeless: Spirituality in the Workweek
by John McQuiston II Simple stories show you how refocus your daily life.
5½ x 6¾, 208 pp, HC, 978-1-59473-035-1 **$17.99**

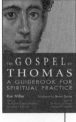

The Gospel of Thomas: A Guidebook for Spiritual Practice
by Ron Miller; Translations by Stevan Davies
6 x 9, 160 pp, Quality PB, 978-1-59473-047-4 **$14.99**

Earth, Water, Fire, and Air: Essential Ways of Connecting to Spirit
by Cait Johnson 6 x 9, 224 pp, HC, 978-1-893361-65-2 **$19.95**

Labyrinths from the Outside In: Walking to Spiritual Insight—A Beginner's Guide
by Donna Schaper and Carole Ann Camp
6 x 9, 208 pp, b/w illus. and photos, Quality PB, 978-1-893361-18-8 **$16.95**

Practicing the Sacred Art of Listening: A Guide to Enrich Your Relationships
and Kindle Your Spiritual Life—The Listening Center Workshop
by Kay Lindahl 8 x 8, 176 pp, Quality PB, 978-1-893361-85-0 **$16.95**

Releasing the Creative Spirit: Unleash the Creativity in Your Life
by Dan Wakefield 7 x 10, 256 pp, Quality PB, 978-1-893361-36-2 **$16.95**

The Sacred Art of Bowing: Preparing to Practice
by Andi Young 5½ x 8½, 128 pp, b/w illus., Quality PB, 978-1-893361-82-9 **$14.95**

The Sacred Art of Chant: Preparing to Practice
by Ana Hernández 5½ x 8½, 192 pp, Quality PB, 978-1-59473-036-8 **$15.99**

The Sacred Art of Fasting: Preparing to Practice
by Thomas Ryan, CSP 5½ x 8½, 192 pp, Quality PB, 978-1-59473-078-8 **$15.99**

The Sacred Art of Forgiveness: Forgiving Ourselves and Others through God's Grace
by Marcia Ford 8 x 8, 176 pp, Quality PB, 978-1-59473-175-4 **$16.99**

The Sacred Art of Listening: Forty Reflections for Cultivating a Spiritual Practice
by Kay Lindahl; Illustrations by Amy Schnapper
8 x 8, 160 pp, b/w illus., Quality PB, 978-1-893361-44-7 **$16.99**

The Sacred Art of Lovingkindness: Preparing to Practice
by Rabbi Rami Shapiro; Foreword by Marcia Ford 5½ x 8½, 176 pp, Quality PB, 978-1-59473-151-8 **$16.99**

Sacred Speech: A Practical Guide for Keeping Spirit in Your Speech
by Rev. Donna Schaper 6 x 9, 176 pp, Quality PB, 978-1-59473-068-9 **$15.99**
HC, 978-1-893361-74-4 **$21.95**

About SKYLIGHT PATHS Publishing

SkyLight Paths Publishing is creating a place where people of different spiritual traditions come together for challenge and inspiration, a place where we can help each other understand the mystery that lies at the heart of our existence.

Through spirituality, our religious beliefs are increasingly becoming a part of our lives—rather than *apart* from our lives. While many of us may be more interested than ever in spiritual growth, we may be less firmly planted in traditional religion. Yet, we do want to deepen our relationship to the sacred, to learn from our own as well as from other faith traditions, and to practice in new ways.

SkyLight Paths sees both believers and seekers as a community that increasingly transcends traditional boundaries of religion and denomination—people wanting to learn from each other, *walking together, finding the way.*

For your information and convenience, at the back of this book we have provided a list of other SkyLight Paths books you might find interesting and useful. They cover the following subjects:

Buddhism / Zen	Global Spiritual	Monasticism
Catholicism	Perspectives	Mysticism
Children's Books	Gnosticism	Poetry
Christianity	Hinduism /	Prayer
Comparative	Vedanta	Religious Etiquette
Religion	Inspiration	Retirement
Current Events	Islam / Sufism	Spiritual Biography
Earth-Based	Judaism	Spiritual Direction
Spirituality	Kabbalah	Spirituality
Enneagram	Meditation	Women's Interest
	Midrash Fiction	Worship

Or phone, fax, mail or e-mail to: SKYLIGHT PATHS Publishing
Sunset Farm Offices, Route 4 • P.O. Box 237 • Woodstock, Vermont 05091
Tel: (802) 457-4000 • Fax: (802) 457-4004 • www.skylightpaths.com
Credit card orders: (800) 962-4544 (8:30AM–5:30PM ET Monday–Friday)
Generous discounts on quantity orders. SATISFACTION GUARANTEED. Prices subject to change.

For more information about each book,
visit our website at www.skylightpaths.com